Breakthrough Declarations Of A Praying Wife

How To Speak Life And Love Into Your Family

Julian Businge

Greatness University Publishers
info@greatness-university.com
www.greatness-university.com

ISBN: 978-1-9993481-2-0
ISBN-13: 978-1-9993481-2-0

DEDICATION

This book is dedicated to my husband and children with whom we walk together in our journey of faith to discover God's will for us. Thank you all for allowing me to make a positive contribution to society.

CONTENTS

ACKNOWLEDGMENTS

All praise, honour and glory to my Lord Jesus Christ for His richest grace and mercy for the accomplishment of this book. This book has been written from the inspiration of the Holy Spirit.

I also acknowledge the cooperation and support I have received through many individuals right from the beginning of my journey as an author. First and foremost, my sincere thanks to Dr. Patrick Businge, my lovely husband, the Founder of Greatness University Publishers for his time, support, encouragement and expertise to make this book.

I wish to express my deep gratitude to my children Stella and Eric, you are my eternal treasures in my heart. I regret any time we argued in front of you, before we learned that prayer is more powerful than yelling in anger. I pray for you, that when you grow older and are ready for marriage, you will carry all the good and positives that you have learned into your own marriages.

To my beautiful mother Mrs Lucy Sabiiti, my precious siblings, relatives, in laws, pastors and friends,am eternally indebted to you all for being a wonderful inspiration and encouragement and support to me. I am also grateful to Delphia Cuddye who added meaning to my ideas. Special thanks to all the men and women of God standing in prayer with us. God Bless you all.

Julian Businge

PREFACE

I will never forget the day I got married. This day brought me much joy, reward and a sense of great achievement. I am so grateful God heard my prayer and brought my husband Patrick into my life. Thank you God for my family. I prayed and dreamed of the day I would find my soulmate and start a family.

During those days when single, I gave little thought to learning about marriage and all that was involved in having a successful marriage. I never imagined any struggles and conflict we might face on this journey. I guess it was all because I watched a lot of Romeo and Juliet movies. I hope you relate with me.

We got married after a few months of long distance relationship and later I joined my husband in UK. Our first year was amazing as we were both adjusting and getting to know each other more. I don't think it crossed my mind that God would use my marriage to make me more like Christ.

I knew I had to learn to be humble etc. I never thought God would reveal so many of my flaws. I have learnt my lessons now. After talking to so many people in need of prayer, I have discovered that I am not the only one who has experienced this reality. The good news is that God changes hearts starting with me. When the attitude of Christ begins to consume us, we become the loving, supportive, caring person towards our spouse and others too. It takes the challenges and the pain of marriage to reveal the truth about our hearts. We are all sinners in the process of being redeemed.

In sharing my journey, I and my husband have traveled through brokenness to a place of peace and comfort and we are still learning and growing together, its not yet over. The process is not yet finished, but it is going on. This is not the end, but it is the road. Usually when two non-related adults suddenly choose to occupy the same space to stay together, it takes time to adjust and will have issues along the way but when it happens something has to give in. That something needs to be our immaturity, pride and self-centeredness. It all has to go out and never return in Jesus' name for marriage to work out.

Whether you are newly married or engaged, we all have issues in our homes. My prayer is that God will use breakthrough declarations of a praying wife as a tool to encourage you, to inspire you and to help you interpret the events of your life for a positive turn around.

Prayer Point

Dear Lord, I am grateful for my family, my joys, my sorrows and for all that has made us stronger in our marriage. We give you God our father all the praise and glory for you doing something new and beautiful in our lives everyday. We are moving from strength to strength and from victory to victory in every area of our lives.

O Holy Spirit , help us to remember that we don't know everything, but that you are our counselor who understands it all and is at work in our family. Open our minds to understand your truths and learn to trust in you always. Without you, nothing is impossible, and you work everything according to what is good, right and timely.

O Holy Spirit, You are the healer and comforter, heal us physically, spiritually and emotionally of all the pains, hurts, wounds, sufferings, sorrows, trials, difficulties that we have faced. Help us to recognize your presence and turn to you in ALL situations. You promised to never leave us nor abandon us. You are working a plan for our benefit, to make good come from everything that happens to us. In Jesus' name, Amen.

Julian Businge

INTRODUCTION

One of the easiest ways to achieve a breakthrough is to speak what the word of God says in his promises while in prayer. The word of God is life. It is alive and active sharper than any double edged sword. Use it to speak love and life into your family every day.

When we do this, we align our desires and perspectives with His, which brings spiritual breakthrough. Marriage is a gift from God and is to be used for his glory in expressions of pure delight. Marriage is meant to be heaven on earth. When the two become one. It is God's idea of family setting in the garden of Eden.

I put together this practical little book, packed with prayers, declarations commonly known as affirmations, wisdom and tips that will help many develop the loving, supportive and mutually beneficial marriage men and women long for. This is not a book simply to be read. It is a book to be experienced.

In this book, information is provided that will keep both husband and wife on equal footing and equally satisfied by using a prayer strategy called declaring and affirming praise and appreciation. As you take notice of your husband, he will feel valued and respected and do the same for you. This is a win-win team. When your husband wins, the wife wins too, the couple's love for one another actually grows and is sustained for the rest of their lives with this tool.

Proverbs 31:10 says, 'An excellent wife, who can find? For her worth is far above jewels'. Achieving breakthrough in your marriage is not for the weak, meek, sensitive, passive or faint of heart. You must go after your spiritual, physical, financial and mental freedom aggressively, passionately and strategically. You must be prepared to pray the daring prayers necessary to set yourself free and all your family from every form captivity to obtain the point of your desired breakthrough.

Overview

Treat your marriage like you would anything of the utmost importance, work on it daily, weekly and monthly. It is like a plant, nurture it well. Happy relationships are integral to our health, success at work / business and peace in the home.

This book is a gentle tool of restoration to women who desire to pray and get results for their husbands and children. A wife who longs to do right more than be right, and to give life in every possible way. She uses the power of the tongue to speak words of love and life into her family. It's a way to invite God's power into your husband's life for his greatest blessing, which is ultimately yours, too. It is not a means of gaining control over your husband and children but learning to pray for others, relying on God's power to transform you, your husband, your children and circumstances.

Praying for your husband is an act of unselfish, unconditional love and sacrifice on wives who wish to enjoy heaven on earth. You must be willing to make this commitment no matter the situation or circumstance you're in with your husband. The strength of a man and wife joined together in God's sight is far greater than the sum of the strengths of each of the two individuals. That's because the Holy Spirit unites them and gives added power to their prayers. They are a team, one unit, unified in spirit.

If you pray for yourself and not him, you will never find the blessings and fulfilment you want. What happens to him happens to you and you can't get around it. Trust in God to take away the pain, hopelessness, hardness, and un-forgiveness you have been encountering. This oneness gives us a power that the enemy doesn't like. That is why he devises ways to weaken it. He gives us whatever we will fall for, whether it be low self-esteem, pride, the need to be right, miscommunication, or the bowing to our own selfish desires or jealousy. The devil will tell you lies like, "Nothing will ever change." "Your failures are irreparable."

Whenever differences arose between my husband and I, praying was definitely not my first thought. In fact, it was closer to a last resort. I tried other methods first such as arguing, ignoring, avoiding, confronting, going to the next room and of course the ever-popular silent treatment, all with far less than satisfying results. It has taken me some time to realize that by praying first, these unpleasant methods of operation could be avoided. I can say without reservation that prayer works. A wife, because of her nearness to her husband, is usually the most powerful human influence in her husband's life.

Am still learning about this and it doesn't come easy. While I may not have as much practice doing it right as I have had doing it wrong, you have to determine that everything consuming you and your husband, such as arguments, domestic abuse, workaholics, alcoholism, drug abuse, or depression, can be destroyed in the name of Jesus. A blisful marriage is your portion from now on. You have to know that whatever has crept into your relationship so silently and stealthily as to not even be perceived as a threat until it is clearly present such as neglecting your husband and making idols of your career, your dreams, your kids, or your selfish desires. The power that resurrected Jesus is the very same power that will resurrect the dead places of your marriage and put life back into it. **Happy Reading...**

Julian Businge

Chapter 1

What is Breakthrough?

Julian Businge

What is a breakthrough?

Are you wondering what breakthrough is all about and why is it vital to you and to your marriage? Breakthrough is really about knowing who we are in God and being willing to take the lead, to go where others have not gone, or broken through into new territories. It is about winning where others have not. It's a change in mindset that its possible to have what you desire in your family no matter what appears to be real. It is about appropriating the victories of Jesus Christ (and all that He did for us), and demonstrating the dominion, power and reality of that victory by living our lives daily to his glory.

Having a relationship with Jesus starts with a breakthrough such as a breakthrough from a life of sin to forgiveness. His grace breaks the power of that sin! That relationship with Jesus transforms us in such a way that we are now able to accomplish things that we have never been able to before. Not by power nor might but by his Spirit, says the Lord, we gain access to the dominon and power against the powers of darkness through Jesus. He is the way, the truth and the life.

Breakthrough is experiencing:

- Life instead of death. Jesus came that we might have life in abundance
- Righteousness instead of sin
- Grace instead of law and legislation

- Reality instead of religion
- Regeneration instead of degeneration
- Functioning in the Holy Spirit's anointing instead of our own natural ability
- Love instead of fear
- Active faith instead of dead works
- Joy instead of sadness
- Victory instead of defeat
- Knowing God's provision instead of poverty
- Being "the head and not the tail" (Deuteronomy 28:13)
- Being fruitful instead of being fruitless
- Knowing we belong in God's family, of "being accepted in the beloved" (Ephesians 1:6), instead of living in rejection
- A positive life-style instead of a negative one.

It is not a matter of propagating theories of the Christian life – it is demonstrating that it works, and that it works effectively. There is no victory "without" until first we win the victory "within"! The key to make a breakthrough in the Christian life is that we must first breakthrough in ourselves! We show the way, how it is done, and lead by example.

Breakthrough is not for those who will never attempt anything new or different or outside which is easily attainable. The sad reality is that many of those who say they believe in Jesus are not enjoying breakthrough in their lives. They have not yet overcome themselves in such a way that they can rise out of their negativities, past circumstances, hurts, sin, whatever it was that knocked them back.

Breakthrough is all about rising above those negativities, criticisms, failures, and showing that we do not have to be bound by the past, but through Jesus Christ and His mighty Holy Spirit we have a glorious present and future to grasp a hold of. All we have to do is **BREAKTHROUGH** whatever it is that is keeping us back and stuck in life.

YOU CAN DO IT!

There is no future in the past. The past is gone. Today is here, the new has come and God wants us to live today in such a way that we will breakthrough into a future that is far better than anything we have ever accomplished before.

No spiritual breakthrough is greater or more important than receiving salvation by faith in Christ and what He did on the cross for us. It is through his sacrifice on the cross we are reconciled to God. Without the shedding of His blood, there is no remission of our sins (Hebrews 9:22). God didn't give everything for us in His Son because there are other ways.

We cannot experience the other breakthroughs God has for us until we first receive and believe in Jesus. We do this by calling on His Name to save us. You confess with your mouth and believe in your heart that Jesus is Lord (Romans 10:13). St Paul says that

"Our struggle is not against flesh and blood, but against the rulers, against the authorities, against the powers of this dark world and against the spiritual forces of evil in the heavenly realms." Ephesians 6:12. Often the spiritual breakthroughs we need is brought about through prayer and fasting, not by asking favors of people, or pushing for our own way. Stop looking to people for your breakthrough, and start storming the gates of heaven through prayer. Ask and it shall be given unto you.

Prayer Point

Dear God, make us sober-minded, watchful and clothed with Your protective armour in our home, that we may be able to stand against the plans of the devil.

- Father Lord, by your mighty power, scatter and destroy any hindering spirit to our progress in all areas of our lives around us in our marriage.
- Evil decree or curse over our family, spiritually,physically,financially, matrimonially, and educationally, I break your hold, in the name of Jesus, we are free from now onwards.
- Lord Jesus may your plan and purpose for my marriage come to pass in Jesus' name.
- My father, my maker, let every cord of darkness, militating against my breakthroughs catch fire now in Jesus name.
- Every lying and accusing tongue against me or any member of my family I command you to be silenced by the blood of Jesus.
- God, araise and laugh at the plot of the wicked fashioned against our marriage in the name of Jesus.

- God our father may your will alone for our family prosper in our lives, let every barriers, obstacles,prayerlessness against our destines be consumed by the fire of the Holy Spirit in Jesus' name
- Every setup for a setback by the enemy against my family, back to the sender in Jesus' name.
- Father, let the hedge of thorns surround me and my family, in the name of Jesus.

The Importance of Breakthrough

Each person has a clear definition of breakthrough, it is personal and very specific. To some people, breakthrough might be salvation. To others, it might be freedom from debt. To another, it might be throwing off the chains of fear and to another having a united family. The list of possibilities is never-ending. But with the power of the Lord, that which binds you or your loved one, it is not never-ending.

The strongest way to combat chains and achieve breakthrough is by the truth of God's Word. As John 8:32 says, it is the truth of the Scripture – the very words of God – that sets us free. Chains fall when we cling to the hope of God's promises. Breakthrough happens when we seek God's will and rest our confidence in Him. In addition, prayer is a powerful weapon against that which holds us captive. When we pray the truth of Scripture, we claim the promises of God by releasing them back to Him. "The effectual fervent prayer of a righteous man availeth much" (James 5:16). The prayers we say bring great breakthrough in our lives because of the power and dominon given to us.

The things which hold us captive have no place in our lives. We must surrender anything and everything which holds a place in our heart that God should have. 2 Timothy 1:7 states, "For God has not given us a spirit of fear, but of power and of love and of a sound mind." Breakthrough began there, and will continue. By holding onto the promises of God's Word, you will able to take the steps towards committing that fear to God. Love your husband, children, friends, inlaws etc.

Prayer Point

Ephesians 1:3

- I decree the manifestation of all of God's blessing and favour in my husband and childrens' life in the name of Jesus. Read Father, let your glory shine upon my husbands life and career, in Jesus name.
- As I come in obedience to God and his word, I pray that all the days of difficulties have come to an end in our family and we will spend our days in prosperity and our years in pleasure in the name of Jesus.
Read Job 36: 11.
- Power to succeed in life, come upon my spouse now, in the name of Jesus.
- Power to see and discern, come upon my spouse, in the name of Jesus.
- Power to over-come, fall upon my spouse now, in the name of Jesus.
- I come against every form of worry in his life. Even though things may seem impossible but I pray he will trust and believe that with God nothing shall be impossible.
Read Matthew 19 verse 26.

- Every blessing that Jesus secured on the cross, arise and locate my spouse, in the name of Jesus.

Pray every day and continually give thanks to God and you will surely experience God's breakthrough in your family life. You shall come back with a testimony.

Spiritual Breakthrough

"If you're praying for a breakthrough and not seeing it, do not give up. Opposition precedes breakthroughs. Do you remember the story of the wall of Jericho. The Isrealites had to sing and give praise 7 times around the wall before it fell. Usually breakthroughs are not achieved by prayer alone: there are works to be done and courage to be exercised consistently and persistently as led by the Holy Spirit. Concentrated, specific, persistent, prevailing prayer, often engaged in by two or more people (Matthew 18:19), is needed to weaken our spiritual opposition.

And fasting too is a wonderful weapon to overcome any storm. "Fasting tests where the heart is. And when it reveals that the heart is with God and not the world, a mighty blow is struck against Satan" (A Hunger for God). So if you're praying for a breakthrough and not seeing it, and in fact experiencing more temptations to discouragement, frustration, weariness, doubt, and fear than before, do not give up. Increasingly intense fighting always precedes strategic breakthroughs.

A happy marriage is the central pillar of a satisfying life. Whether it's about making it work with a new partner, just enjoying a newlywed marriage, putting things right after a quarrel, or dealing with insecurity, praying strategically with knowledge of God's promises can really help you deal with the psychological and emotional issues that arise in any marriage situation. "You will also declare a thing and it will be established for you; So light will shine on your ways." (Job 22:28 NKJV). Your words have power. Proverbs 18:21 tells us that death and life are in the power of our tongue: and they that love it shall eat the fruit thereof.

In James 3 we are told our tongue is like a rudder of a ship. Just as a rudder determines the direction of a ship, our words determine the direction of our life. Begin declaring God's Word over your family that you may all be established and experience life and blessings. Chart the course of your life by declaring Gods Word. He has promised to "watch over His Word to perform it" (Jeremiah 1:12). God is not obliged to perform anyone' word. God's Word will accomplish what it is sent to do (Isaiah 55:11).

There are a lot of different things you can choose to say. You can choose to quote great philosophers or the opinions of men, you can choose to speak your own ideas or thoughts, or choose to declare the facts and circumstances you face. You can choose to declare God's Word that is true and has been tested to bring forth results. Don't be overwhelmed by the many ways. There are many ways to pray for your husband and children. It's not necessary to do it all in one day, one week, or even a month. Let the suggestions in this book be a guide and then pray as the Holy Spirit leads you. Where there are tough issues and you need a dynamic breakthrough, fasting will make your prayers more effective. Your words have power. The more you speak them, the more you will see them come to pass. Tell other people good things about your husband and children. It honours him and he will feel loved by you.

In my home we use a tool called magic words. We call them magic because the more you speak them the more they will come to pass in your life. Its basically speaking God's word over our lives before we all go to bed. Each individual has a chance. We get to affirm the words of faith like, I am Blessed, I am healthy, I am protected, God has a good plan for me, etc, I could go on and on. I find that this has helped us to grow in faith as a family and to believe the impossible. When faced with any fear or situation we remind eachother of the magic words.

Julian Businge

Prayer Point

O Lord, deliver us from any strongholds Satan may have in our family because of our sins and those of our ancestors, in Jesus' name.

- Every curse of my father's house, and my mother's house, working against our growth spiritually, emotional and, break, in the mighty name of Jesus.
- Every decree of the enemy to stop us from advancing in every area of our lives, catch fire, in the name of Jesus.
- Every power that wants my family to expire before my testimony, die, in the name of Jesus.
- Any power flying to arrest our miracles and breakthroughs for our home, fall down and die, in the name of Jesus.
- I break all known and unknown bondages in our family with the blood of Jesus.
- I cancel all known and unknown curses by the blood of Jesus to nullify their consequences upon my marriage, in the name of Jesus Christ.

Julian Businge

Chapter 2

What is Declaration?

Julian Businge

What is a declaration?

Are you wondering what declarations are? Its commonly referred to as postivie Affirmations.It is anything we say or think and believe the majority of what we say and think is quite negative. Every thought we think and every word we say is an affirmation to ourselves.

Doing affirmations or declarations sends a message to our subconscious mind letting it know that we are taking responsibility for our life and what we are creating. By doing this daily means saying an affirmation to negate something unpleasant in our life or saying an affirmation to create something pleasant in our life. We have to be aware of our thoughts and eliminate those that are creating experiences that we do not want in our life. Research has shown that to get permanent results, we are advised to use affirmations for a period of 30 days until they permeate our consciousness and become a part of us.

The tools we need to change our lives for the better already exist within us; and these tools are our thoughts and beliefs. This means we have to be very careful with our words, choosing to speak only those which works towards our benefit and cultivate our highest good. Affirmations help purify our thoughts and restructure the dynamic of our brains so that we truly begin to think nothing is impossible. Nothing is impossible to him who believes.

We have not hardwired our brain to experience a reflection of paradise with ultimate peace and love because of the parasite in our mind that keeps the past alive. Every time we think there is no problem, the body and mind conditioned in the past finds a problem.

Christ tried to present us another way of living when he implied to his followers that they should live like nature. He said look at the lilies and the birds. See how they grow with no stress or toil. You can live like that too. The only way we can live like that is through the thoughts we choose to focus on in this moment. In order to live like the lily your thoughts have to be natural and clear like the growth of the lily. We must allow life to flow freely with an attitude of peace and wholeness no matter what the present circumstance. This action creates a reaction of peace in the future.

The karma for a natural flower is natural beauty because it's action and reaction is natural with no distress and rooted in love. It takes in just enough solar energy and water and the roots grow and create beauty on the outside through the creators love. The only thing that gets in the way of us living our lives so peacefully like the lilly and the bird is fear in the human mind. We have to gain control of our subconscious memory system and alter our attention to abundant words of affirmation. We have been conditioned by school for most of our early years so more than likely you have to unlearn some things you've been taught.

Whatever words of affirmation you have planted in your mental garden, will be the same words that grows in your physical world as manifestation of things and reality and now is the time to pluck up roots and plant new seeds. Our minds are like a garden ,we have to plant the right seeds we want to grow and uproot the bad weeds. Then the new seeds of abundance have to become deeply rooted and implicit so that it can be automatic. Peace and love becomes second nature and all other needs are added as a result of producing compassion now.

No words are empty words, as every syllable we speak engages energy towards or against us. If you constantly say "I can't" the energy of your words will repel the universal force against you. But if you say words like "I can!",' its possible' the Lord our creator will endow you with the abilities to do just that. So, keep praying don't give up no matter what, the best will manifest in your marriage.

Begin your day declaring it and then repeat it throughout the day. As you declare these decrees they will be established in your life. Be blessed!

Declarations

The choice is yours and yours alone. I challenge you to choose to declare God's Word. Use the following 31 declarations of God's Word to get started.

• **I DECLARE** I am guided in my every step by the Holy Spirit who leads me towards what I must know and do in my marriage and other areas of my life.

• **I DECLARE** A river of compassion washes away all anger in our home and replaces it with love.

• **I DECLARE** My marriage is becoming stronger, deeper, and more stable each day.

• **I DECLARE**, Today, I abandon my old habits and take up new, more positive habits.

• **I DECLARE** I am blessed with an incredible family and wonderful friends.

• **I DECLARE** I am a child of God, forgiven, and loved by God. I will serve the Lord all the days of my life with gladness. (Romans 8:16; Psalms 100:2)

• **I DECLARE** I hear and follow the voice of the good shepherd and follow not the voice of the stranger. I am doing the right thing, in the right way, and the right time. (John 10:4-5)

• **I DECLARE** that the goodness and mercy of God are following all my loved ones in every day of their lives. They will dwell in the house of the Lord forever. (Psalms 23:6)

• **I DECLARE** my family has favour with God and with man.

. **I DECLARE** ,my family is surrounded with favor like a shield. Now is our time. This is the appointed time of Gods vision for our life to come to pass. (Proverbs 3:4; Psalms 5:12: Habbakuk 2:3)

• **I DECLARE** no weapon formed against me or my family will prosper. His angels have charge over us and no evil will come near me or my home. I fear no evil. (Isaiah 54:17; Psalms 91:11; Psalms 23:4)

• **I DECLARE** I and my spouse have perfect peace in our lives and home. We pursue peace with all people and in every situation. Great is our peace. (Isaiah 26:3; Matthew 5:9; Hebrews 12:14)

• **I DECLARE** I am a winner. My husband is a Winner. My children are winners. The Lord always brings us through and are victorious. (Romans 8:37: 1 Corinthians 15:57)

• **I DECLARE** I am not intimidated by the enemy and I have a sound mind and a spirit of courage and boldness. I am prepared and ready to face every challenge the day brings. (2 Timothy 1:7: Ephesians 3:12)

• **I DECLARE** God is opening the windows of heaven over my life and I am experiencing the abundant life Jesus came to give me. Unexpected blessings are coming my way. (Malachi 3:10: John 10:10b)

• **I DECLARE** all my needs are being met. I am not barely getting by, but I have more than enough. I am able to sow into every good work. (Philppians 4:19: 2 Corinthians 9:8)

• **I DECLARE** I am not weary in doing the good things God has called me to do. I will persevere and overcome. I will reap a harvest on the seeds I have sown at exactly the right time. (Galations 6:9)

• **I DECLARE** I am valuable because of who made me and because of the price Jesus paid for me. I am here for a divine purpose. No one else is like me. I have been fearfully and wonderfully made by God. I am unique, special and extraordinary to God. (Psalms 139:14)

• **I DECLARE** I am forgiven by God. I have no fear, guilt, or condemnation in my life because the Spirit of life in Christ Jesus has made me free from the law of sin and death. I walk in freedom and liberty by the Spirit of God.

• **I DECLARE** I am right with God not because of anything I have done, but because of what Jesus has done. He has taken my sinfulness and given me His righteousness. I am the rightousness of God in Christ Jesus!

• **I DECLARE** that the Spirit of Christ is alive within me, giving me a passion to do things God's way, and delivering me from every bad habit, addiction, and/or vices. I am putting off the old and putting on the new. (Galations 2:20; Ephesians 4:22-24)

• **I DECLARE** that our family leaders,elders and all pastors and those we relate with to ask for guidance will have Godly wisdom, they shall be led by the spirit and love of God and they be covered with the grace and mercy of our Lord Jesus Christ.

Those who are unsaved will be saved by Gods Grace and mercy and the ungodly will be changed or removed, for the will of God to be done in our marriage. (1Timothy 2:2)

• **I DECLARE** I am living by faith and not by sight. I am not moved by what I see or what I feel. I speaking to the obstacles and barriers in my life to be removed. I have the faith of God in me. (2Corinthians 5:7 Mark 11:22-23)

• **I DECLARE** greater is He that lives in me than he who is in the world and that the same Spirit that raised Jesus from the dead is alive in me. (1 John 4:4; Romans 8:11)

• **I DECLARE** I will not worry, I will not doubt, I will keep my trust in the Lord, confident He will not fail me.

• **I DECLARE** I love God because He first loved me! His love for me is unconditional and never changing. There is nothing that can separate me from His love. (1John 4:19: Romans 8:38)

• **I DECLARE** I am receiving an abundant supply of wisdom and understanding from God. I will know how to apply God's word accurately in every situation, circumstance of my life.

• **I DECLARE** I am receiving Godly wisdom.The wisdom of God that is pure, peaceable, gentle, unwavering, willing to yield, without hypocrisy. (James 1:5: James 3:17)

• **I DECLARE** I am receiving supernatural strength and encouragement from God and my angels and they are carrying out the Word of God and every word that I speak that lines up with the Word of God is being carried out by angels, even now as I speak. (Psalm 103:20)

• **I DECLARE** I am FRUITFUL, I MULTIPLY, I REPLENISH, I SUBDUE, and I have Dominion in this world each day of my life!

• **I DECLARE** I will only think on things that are true, honest, just, pure, lovely, and of good report. I cast down vain imaginations and thoughts that are contrary to things of God. My mind is ready and obedient to the Word of God.

• **I DECLARE** satan has no power over me. I have been delivered from the power of darkness and translated into the Kingdom of God's dear Son. (Colossians 1:13)

- **I DECLARE** Every thing that happens to me or around is ultimately working together for good in my life because I love God and I am called according to His purpose. (Romans 8:28)

- **I DECLARE** I am ready for every good work that God has planned for me. I am called and anointed by God to serve Him. I will fulfill my destiny. (2Timothly 3:17)

- **I DECLARE** nothing is lacking, broken or missing in my marriage. We are whole and complete in Christ. (Colossians 2:10)

- **I DECLARE** everything and anything that has been lost or stolen is being restored. I am pursuing, overtaking and getting back everything the enemy has taken in my family. (Joel 2:25; 1Samuel 30:8)

- **I DECLARE** I am the healed of the Lord. I walk in divine health and wholeness. I have a sound mind, strong spirit, and health body.(1Peter 2:24; 2Timothy 1:7)

- **I DECLARE I am Blessed**

- **I DECLARE** I am the head and not the tail.

- **I DECLARE** I will lend to many nations and not borrow. Every thing I put my hand to prospers. (Deuteronomy 28:13)

"So shall My word be that goes forth from my mouth; It shall not return to me void, but it shall accomplish what I please, And it shall prosper in the thing for which I sent it." Isaiah 55:11 NKJV

Many difficult things that happen in a marriage relationship are actually part of the enemy's plan set up for its demise. But we can say:

I refuse the report of the enemy in Jesus Name.

"I will not allow anything to destroy my marriage."

"I will not stand by and watch my husband be wearied, beaten down, or destroyed."

"I will not sit idle while an invisible wall goes up between us."

"I will not allow confusion, miscommunication, wrong attitudes, and bad choices to erode what we are trying to build together."

"I will not tolerate hurt and unforgiveness leading us to divorce." We can take a stand against any negative influences in our marriage relationship and know that God has given us authority in His name to back it up.

You have the means to establish a hedge of protection around your marriage because Jesus said, "Whatever you bind on earth will be bound in heaven, and whatever you loose on earth will be loosed in heaven" (Matthew 18:18). You have authority in the name of Jesus to stop evil and permit good.

You can submit to God in prayer whatever controls your husband like alcoholism, workaholism, laziness, depression, infirmity, abusiveness, anxiety, fear, or failure,no matter the situation; pray for him to be released and set free from bondage by the Lord.

Lastly, it is pointless to ask God for direction if you are not willing to move your feet. Every breakthrough and every success story is the combination of divine power and human effort. God brought manna to Israel, but He didn't make it fall inside their tents, neither did God pick it up and chew it for them.

Exodus 16, states that no amount of praying or fasting could replace Israel's need for decision-making and a decisive action. Each Israelite had to get up early in the morning, find containers and gather enough manna for the day. God will never do for you anything that He's already given you the strength to do.

God wants to bless you financially, but you have to get up every morning and work diligently and faithfully. God wants to bless you with a child, but you have to endure the nine long months of pregnancy. God wants to bless you with a loving husband, but you must get out of your comfort zone, sacrifice comfort and convenience, open your heart to love and be loved, invest time in the relationship, lose a few friends and disappoint some family members along the way.

Just because it is from God doesn't mean it's to be easy. God gave Israel the Promised land but they had to walk through the desert, cross seas and flooded rivers, and fight and kill for it.

Whatever it is that you've been praying for, God might've already said yes. But it won't fall on your lap without your effort and action. After claiming it in prayer you must get up and take it by force. Birds are born to fly, not withstanding the law of gravity. Fish are born to swim, not withstanding the principle of floatation.

Every child of God is born to win the battles of life, regardless of all obstacles and challenges. Whatsoever is born of God overcomes the world. No two birds have ever collided in the sky, which means there's more space for all of them. You don't need to pull your neighbor down to succeed. Pulling someone down does not necessarily mean you will go up! There is more than enough space and resources for us all to be the best that God wants us to be. Blessings to you all.

Prayer Point

Read Ephesian 3 :20

Oh Lord, give me the weapon of war. Let every evil force of darkness that has been stealing away blessings from my family be defeated, by the power of the Holy Ghost.In Jesus Name.

God, I know and believe that you are able to do beyond what I am seeking or asking for, and even beyond anything I can imagine in the name of Jesus. Every power that wants our destiny helpers to die before reaching us, die, in the name of Jesus.

Delayed testimony, delayed breakthrough manifest by fire, in the name of Jesus. Amen

Julian Businge

Chapter 3

A Praying Wife

A Praying Wife

Problems in marriage are inevitable. The question is - can you remain satisfied in your marriage in spite of differences? Can your marriage thrive when there are differences between you? The answer is yes: keeping a positive mindset through prayer.

A praying woman recognizes the fact that the key to successful marriage is to continually work it out and grow up. Acknowledge the problem and talk about it. Your love for each other doesn't have to be overwhelmed by your differences. The followings are the principales of a praying woman.

A praying woman believes that, God is the only one who should have power over her soul. She follows Gods instructions in whatever she do, that is the reason the marriage is always successful.

God directs a family through a praying woman. She does not leave her relationships to chance. She pray for godly people to come into her life with whom she can connect. She doesn't force relationships to happen. She prays for them to happen and nurture it with prayer.

A praying woman rejoices always. She prays without ceasing. For everything she gives thanks to God.

A praying woman tells God if she is angry at her husband. She doesn't let it become a cancer that grows with each passing day. She doesn't say, "I'm going to live my life and let him live his." There's a price to pay when we act entirely independently of one another. "Neither is man independent of woman, nor woman independent of man, in the Lord" (1 Corinthians 11:11).

A praying woman always says "Lord, forgive me and create in me a clean heart and right spirit before You. Give me a new, positive, joyful, loving, forgiving attitude toward him". Where he has erred, reveal it to him and convict his heart about it. Lead him through the paths of repentance and deliverance. Help me not to hold myself apart from him emotionally, mentally, or physically because of unforgiveness. Where either of us needs to ask forgiveness of the other, help us to do so.

A praying woman, instead of getting angry, will tell God: "If there is something I'm not seeing that's adding to this problem, reveal it to me and help me to understand it. Remove any wedge of confusion that has created misunderstanding or miscommunication. Where there is behavior that needs to change in either of us, I pray You would enable that change to happen. As much as I want to hang on to my anger toward him because I feel it's justified, I want to do what You want. I release all those feelings to You. Give me a renewed sense of love for him and words to heal this situation."

I could come up with a long list of good things that can come about when you start covering your husband in prayer, but let me just cite a few:

- Your husband will be blessed.
- Your marriage will be blessed.
- Your children and generations to come will be blessed.
- You will be blessed.
- You will bless others with the testimony of your marriage and family life.

It may sound corny or cliché but it's true. Once you begin to ask for God's grace to have a fulfilling marriage and to move in your husband's life, the blessings will come. I am not saying that your marriage and family life will become perfect, nor will your trials, challenges and problems disappear overnight. But believe me, the difficulties of life will become easier to bear.

So, how do we begin praying for our husbands? Here are a few tips, from a wife who is a "non-expert"but is journeying in faith towards a better prayer life: Make a decision to be prayerful or at least pray more than you usually do. Many of us struggle with finding time to pray amidst our hectic schedules. Still, we would be more blessed and blissful if we chose to find time to pray.

We can start with just five minutes a day, then work our way up. We can even inject prayer into our daily routines - when we're doing chores, when we're working, when we're playing with the kids, etc. It's a special time and one has to be committed to see its results.

Prayer Point

- Every power that has condemned me, accused me or pronounced my name in shrines or any other evil altars, I command you to catch fire and be terminated in the name of Jesus.
- Any power circulating my family name to native doctors to terminate us, I command you to backfire and be destroyed in Jesus Name.
- Any wicked mouth confessing my defeat and failure, your days are numbered, scatter and die, in the name of Jesus Christ.
- Any power declaring that I and my husband will not make it, may it catch fire in Jesus' name
- Any power declaring that I will not succeed, you are a liar. I command you to fall down and die, in the name of Jesus Christ!
- The Anointing is increasing in my life and every stubborn york is broken.

Praying For Your Husband

Christian wives have been given the authority and power to stand as an intercessor in the family. We have a responsibility as Christian wives to be helpers to our husbands and part of that means praying for them every day.

Confess your faults one to another, and pray one for another that ye may be healed. The effectual fervent prayer of a righteous man availeth much (James 5:16). Praying for our husbands is a life changing and powerful encouragement for them. Every day, we should be praying especially when we are fighting or irritated with them. This is the BEST time to pray for them if the prayer is for them and not about them!

What causes us to pray ABOUT them instead of FOR them? I mean, many times when we are upset with our husbands, we ask God to fix their issues instead of asking God to bless them.

Back to Causes of problems in marriage

- Unforgiveness

- Bitterness

- Selfishness

- Pride

- Denial

- Unrealistic expectations

We are all fallen. Our husbands are not perfect and never will be. They will ALWAYS let us down in one way or another. That is just the way it is. Am very sure we as wives have let them down too in so many ways. A great way to see how God focused you and and where you are in your personal relationship with Him is to do a self check. What do I mean? Let me explain. We all have had some sort of unrealistic expectation in our marriages. This world makes it very difficult for a wife to have a REALISTIC view of what a husband should be.

Worldly Perspective:

- Husband should buy chocolates and flowers
- Husband should meet all my needs
- Husband should be romantic and sweep me off my feet
- Husband should love me no matter how fat I get
- Husband should remember everything
- Husband should read my mind

God's Word Perspective:

- Wife is to be a helpmate to her husband.
- Wife is to love and forgive her husband.
- Wife is to honour and respect her husband
- Wife is to pray for her husband
- Wife is to seek God too

If you see that you have a more worldly view and feel let down by your husband, you may need to get on your knees more for your husband. You may also need to seek God and develop a personal relationship with Him.

Being a Christian wife is more than believing Jesus died on the Cross and rose on the third day. It is a lifestyle. It is a daily dying of self. It is growing. It is seeking God daily. It is developing a RELATIONSHIP with your Father in Heaven.

Prayer Point

Father I also pray for my husband today and ask that you would help us and our marriage grow stronger by your word. Help us to communicate effectively and grant us the ability to listen to each other with an open heart and mind.

Work Life

I DECLARE My husband works with all his heart as unto the Lord. He glorifies God with his talents. (Colossians 3:23)

I DECLARE The favour of God rests on my husband. God establishes the work of his hands and provides the business he needs. (Psalm 90:17)

Father, thank you for my husband's job. Lord, help him to see it as a gift from You. Father, I pray that you continue to bless him in this area. Give him insight into his field. Continue to show him creative ways to make money and expand his presence in his industry.

Lord, help him to see his job as a blessing, even in tough times. Guard his heart and mind from discouragement when things don't go the way he anticipates. Let him work with all his heart to bring You glory. I pray Your favor would cover him and that he would prosper in his work. In Jesus' name, Amen.

Home Life

I DECLARE My husband leads me with gentleness and walks in understanding with me. (1 Peter 3:7)

I DECLARE My husband is an encouraging father. He leads our children in the way of the Lord. (Ephesians 6:4)

Lord, protect my husband's time at home. Father, help him to govern our house in wisdom and fear of You. Teach him Your ways that He may be an example to our children. Give him insight into how to raise our family. Help him to balance his time between work and home life.

Help him to understand how to love me better as his wife and help me learn to be respectful. Teach us to be gentle and kind with our family while teaching us to be submissive. In Jesus' name, Amen.

Relationships

I DECLARE The wise will surround my husband and he will become wiser. (Proverbs 13:20)

I DECLARE My husband speaks what is edifying to those around him. He builds others up and uses his words to glorify God. (Ephesians 4:29)

I DECLARE My husband is an example to others in speech, in conduct, in love, in faith and in purity. (1 Timothy 4:12)

Father thank you for my husband's godly relationships. Lord continue to surround him with men that reflect Your heart. Help him to be slow to speak and very quick to listen with his friends. Guard his mouth from speaking anything other than what edifies the hearer and glorifies You. Give him divine connections throughout his day. Let him be a beacon of light to those around him. In Jesus' name, Amen.

Physical Health

I DECLARE My husband will be in good health and prosper even as his soul prospers. (3 John 1:2)

My husband is disciplined in his eating and exercising habits. He maintains control over all cravings. (1 Corinthians 9:27)

Lord I thank you for my husband's health. Father I pray that you would preserve him. Help him to make good food choices each day.

Let him crave those things that are good for him. Protect each cell in his body, that nothing harmful can prosper against him.

Give him energy at the end of the day to work out. Show him a plan for working out. Send others to encourage him and even a buddy to work out with that will keep him accountable. In Jesus' name, Amen.

Spiritual Growth

I DECLARE My husband grows in the grace and knowledge of Jesus Christ daily. (2 Peter 3:18)

I DECLARE The faith my husband has will move mountains and nothing will be impossible for him! (Matthew 17:20)

God I thank you that my husband is growing in wisdom, stature and favor with You and man. Continue to expand his knowledge of You, Lord. I thank you for the men you have placed in his life to help him along the way.

Lord, continue to increase his faith as he reads Your Word. Preserve his time with you, Lord. Speak to him throughout the day and guide his decisions. In Jesus' name, Amen.

How do you pray for your husband? Do you have a routine or a specific method for praying for him? I would love for you to share it! We can help each other grow in our efforts to pray for our spouses. The more we pray, declare and seek God on behalf of our men, the more we will see them grow in the image of God.

A Wife Of Noble Character

Some people have a mistaken vision that the ideal Christian wife is weak and feeble: a domestic servant so to speak. But the Bible clearly describes a different picture of a Christian wife. It may surprise you to see that physical appearance is not mentioned at all. But her attractiveness comes from her character as her beauty shines through from the inside.

The following verses describe a picture of Christian womanhood for there is no way anybody could do all of things mentioned below. Most of all it is a guide, because some of the things you will be good at and some you won't. For example you may not have any interest in planting a flower garden or buying property but you may be a wonderful mother and have a special gift in this area. The main idea is to focus on what you are good at, and then be the best you can be in your area of strength in order to honor God's glory.

In Proverbs 31:10-17 NIV it states:

> (10) A wife of noble character who can find? She is worth far more than rubies.
> (11) Her husband has full confidence in her and lacks nothing of value.
> (12) She brings him good, not harm all the days of her life.
> (13) She selects wool and flax and works

with eager hands.

(14) She is like the merchant ships, bringing her food from afar.

(15) She gets up while it is still dark; she provides food for her family portions for her servant girls.

(16) She considers a field and buys it; out of her earnings she plants a vineyard.

(17) She sets about her work vigorously; her arms are strong for her tasks.

(18) She sees that her trading is profitable and her lamp does not go out at night.

(19) In her hand she holds the distaff and grasps the spindle with her fingers.

(20) She opens her arms to the poor and extends her hands to the needy.

(21) When it snows, she has no fear for her household; for all of them are clothed in scarlet.

(22) She makes coverings for her bed; she is clothed in fine linen and purple.

(23) Her husband is respected at the city gate, where he takes his seat among the elders of the land.

The Willingness to be Submissive

The book of Ephesians says "Wives submit to your husbands". According to God's word, a Christian husband is the spiritual leader of the family. If the husband is doing all he can to be like Christ and loving his wife like Christ loved the church, he is standing in his calling and therefore the wife has to stand in her place of submission to have a successful marriage. Actually Paul devotes twice as many words in Ephesians to husbands loving their wives then he does to wives submitting to their husbands. He should make her well being his primary focus. He should love her just as he loves his own body.

Prayer Point

Dear Heavenly Father,

I humbly come before you and ask for your guidance today. I ask that through the Holy Spirit you would show me how to become a better Christian wife just as you have called me to be. Help me to understand what it means to be submissive in a Christian marriage according to your word.

Show me father my strengths as a Christian woman and how I can use those strengths to your glory.

I raise the blood of Jesus as a banner, in the name of Jesus.

My adversaries hear the word of the Lord carry your load, in the name of Jesus.

Julian Businge

A Faithful Wife

A wife is the complementary personality of her husband. She balances up his life; she is not his opposite for if she was to be his opposite it will mean that if the man is good, she will be bad and vice versa.

A wife is connected to her husband in all things and at all times. She is attached to her husband emotionally, sexually and other ways. She is a gift to the man from God for it is written that "he who finds a wife finds a good thing and obtains favour from the Lord." (Proverbs 18:22). The wife should be there for the husband and family in general.

A faithful wife adapts, submits, respects and reveres her husband. She also notices her spouse, honours him and prefers him in all things. She is a blessing to her King! And can go all the way to esteem, praise, love and admire him exceedingly.

The man is the head of the union and 4 out of the 5

senses a human being has are resident in the head. The sense to taste, see, hear, smell are all found in the head and only the sense of feeling is found in the body. As such, the head does the bulk of the work in the union. He does the reasoning while the woman has the feeling.

A faithful wife does not undermine her husband's position; she carries her functions which is complimentary. She prays for her husband; yielding to him always. She loves him, and adores him without reservation. Marital relationship is what Christ and the Church share; the faithful wife always takes clues from how the Church relates with Christ.

It should be noted that men love and adore who they serve and who serves them but are always at logger heads with one on same plane with them. This is why the faithful praying wife always has her way with her husband because she serves her husband and does not try to rub shoulders with him. Remember that submission is not akin to slavery. In slavery, you are forced to do things; a slave has no will of her own. She is coerced into doing things whether she enjoys them or not. Submission is done and born out of love and devotion. But, the faithful wife submits because she admires, adores and appreciates her husband excessively.

A faithful wife trusts her husband irrespective of stories, rumours, gossips and gists from the grapevine. She has and keeps building on her implicit trust in her husband. She believes in him and believes in him totally. The faithful wife doesn't take things for granted. Her dressing is gorgeous and moderate not immodest. She realizes she is married and not single; she dresses to portray honour and respect. Her husband is proud of her and expresses same. She does not keep wrong companies but rather moves with people who influence her positively not those who encourage infidelity and unfaithfulness. She has no hidden secrets and agenda, her husband is uppermost in all her dealings.

The faithful wife is also a virtuous woman and a praying mother combined, she is a complete woman. She studies materials that are relevant to her relationship with her husband; she plans for the future with her husband. She does not drive her man into the waiting arms of the likes of Potiphar's wife. She is not moved by what the man drives but what drives the man. She cherishes and nourishes her times of intimacy with her husband; she holds back nothing in satisfying her man. She is proud of who she married knowing that her husband is her glory and her shield. She does not discuss his weak points but brings her strength to complement those areas.

The faithful wife is a master communicator and a mind reader. She knows what her husband needs per time and does all she could to satisfy his needs. The heart of her man indicts good matters concerning her, she blooms and blossoms because of her role and character. Amidst all charms and lures from detractors, she remains faithful.

Prayer Point

Father, in any area of my life and stewardship that l have fallen short of Your standard and glory, please, forgive me.

Father, without You, I can achieve nothing. Please, empower me to become the faithful and submissive wife to my husband. Together may we succeed and prosper as your servants in all that You have assigned us to do. In Jesus' name.

Father, my maker, help me to be diligent and faithful in all my services to You and be faithful to my family. Give me the grace to do Your work according to your instructions and specifications, that your name may be glorified in me. Take us from Glory to Glory. In Jesus' name.

The Angry And Contentious Wife

Marriage is a school from which no spouse ever graduates until death. This is because marriage as a divinely created institution is a lifelong contract between two persons a man and a woman- who have agreed to live together as husband and wife till death do them part. Marriage is a two-way contract between a man and a woman. It is also a three-some covenant between the man, the woman and God the creator.

Of all human relationships, marriage is the most unique form which God brings together two personalities from different social, spiritual, intellectual and emotional backgrounds. Psalm 139:14 says that man is fearfully and wonderfully created which means that there are no two persons that are exactly alike. It takes much time to be able to learn and accommodate the other spouse's likes and dislikes, tastes and preferences. It takes the grace of God, knowledge and wisdom to adjust and blend in with the differences for a harmonious co-existence.

In marriage, there is always something new to learn and the marriage curriculum can never be exhausted. No one knows it all except God. For the spouses, the more they learn and can apply the better for the marriage. This part of the chapter is directed at the angry and contentious wife (Proverbs 21:19) who makes unkind and derogatory remarks about her husband in the presence of neighbours, friends and relations. She tramples on her husband's self-esteem at will and sets in motion an ugly chain of reactions which she may not be able to reverse later and may spell doom for the marriage.

No reasonable husband can place any iota of trust in a contentious wife unlike the virtuous woman described in Proverbs 31:10-31. A man's self-esteem is his image, his pride and his idea of how the world sees him. It is a man's sense of worth before others. It is his sense of respect which he enjoys from others. A wife who damages her husband's self-esteem does incalculable damage which may cause the death of the marriage over time.

Many husbands may not bother about what a wife says or does as long as their ego is not hurt. Many husbands (Christians and non-Christians) will not take it kindly with any woman who tramples on their self-esteem. No man or husband is perfect as all men (including women) have faults and shortcomings. Many husbands have shortcomings in the social, marital, spiritual, intellectual and financial arena.

How should a wife react to a husband's failings in marriage? There are four ways that women adopt when reacting:

1) Some refuse to talk preferring to nurse a grudge against the husband. This can cause great pressure and distress later on. The husband is completely in the dark about the problem.

2) Some become rude but without discussing the problem with the husband who does not know. This irritates him and he may draw wrong conclusions which may worsen the matter.

3) Some will deliberately hurt the husband via verbal attacks on his person with the intent to humiliate him before others. This method eventually will destroy the home and the marriage if not checked.

4) The wise wife will talk about the issues while taking care not to trample on her husband's self-esteem. This is good communication strategy that enhances harmony and promotes peaceful coexistence in the marriage.

The unwise wife, who is the angry and contentious woman, tramples on her husband's ego in the following ways:

- Nagging and embarrassing him before others
- Speaking to him roughly in the presence of his relations
- Deliberately violating his instructions in order to spite him
- Saying the truth but with the wrong approach as follows: Choosing the wrong time to say it (when), Choosing the wrong location to say it (where), and Choosing the wrong medium to say it (how).

The above characteristics of the angry and contentious woman/wife are a breach of biblical guidelines and instructions on relationship with others. The Bible expressly teaches Christians not to engage in the following sinful practices:
- Destroying one another (Galatians 5:15)
- Provoking one another (Galatians 5:26)
- Slandering one another (James 4:11)
- Grumbling against one another (James 5:9)
The above, known as the negative 'one anothers' create disunity and is evidence of the sinful nature that we are expected to do away with.

The Bible teaches us to forbear with one another in the following ways:
- To honor one another (Romans 12:10)
- To love one another (Romans 13:8)
- To accept one another (Romans 15:7)

- To care for one another (1 Corinthians 12:25)
- To carry one another's burdens (Galatians 6:2)
- To bear with one another (Ephesians 4:2)
- To encourage one another (1 Thessalonians 4:18)
- To pray for one another (James 5:16)
- To submit to one another (Ephesians 5:21).

Therefore, the wife is advised to take the following steps to address her husband's shortcomings:

Communication

Never disobey a husband's instructions because to do so is to hurt him. He will see it as a challenge and will want to assert his authority. However, a wife is not bound to comply with instructions that are a clear violation of God's Word. Discuss issues with him with an attitude of politeness and humility. Discuss with him in the right mood i.e. when he is happy and in a private place. Present your worries and opinions lovingly and carefully, using the right choice of words and taking care not to force your opinions on him.

Submission

If he refuses to see your point, submit to his view. If he finds out later that he is in the wrong and you are in the right, he will respect your opinion and begin to abide by it. But if he refuses to see your point and you also refuse to submit, he will likely see it as an affront on his authority. Even when he knows that you are right, he may not consider your opinions because you were insubordinate.

Helpmate

I said this earlier that a wife is a helper. Genesis 2:18 And the LORD God said, [It is] not good that the man should be alone; I will make him an help meet for him. It may not be possible to change a man when he has become a husband. The wife as a helpmate is expected to complement her husband and protect his interests. Cover up his deficiencies, not exposing him to public ridicule. A true helpmeet will not be scouting for faults when she also has hers which Christ overlooked.

Love

Where there is no love or where love is thin, faults are thick. Before the marriage, love has eyes and can see but after the wedding, love becomes blind and cannot see faults. Marriage is adjustment and acceptance. Overlook his faults and focus more on his strengths and potentials. Love is a decision. You can love the unlovable even when it is not convenient. Encourage him, respect him, stand by him, pray for him and counsel him. Be a dependable woman to him, not a 'broadcaster' of his weaknesses. Pray for the grace to be the woman behind his success. Pray to be a pillar behind him and not a caterpillar that destroys.

Prayer Point

Thank You, Father for the gift of Jesus and His perfect example of humility. Jesus displayed His love for us with great humility and submissiveness to You.

He denied Himself the comforts of heaven to save us. He chose to experience temptations, mockery, rejection, and even death. He rated our needs higher than His own.

Father help me to love, obey, and cherish my husband. Take away the spirit of prideness in me and help me to be a good wife to my darling husband in Jesus' name.

Julian Businge

Chapter 4

Dealing with Marriage Difficulties

Julian Businge

Why Marriages Fail

This section explores a few things that cause marriages to fail and tips to avoid them. 50% of all failed marriages are caused by friction over finances. Communication issues and unrealistic or unmet expectations. Other causes of failed marriages include unfaithfulness, personality clashes, male and female differences, sexual problems and family of origin issues.

The best way to avoid being caught by one of these issues is to educate yourself and become more aware of all of the causes of the issue especially the financial issues of your family. Learn how to be a better communicating couple and spend some time exploring your expectations and your husband's expectations in the marriage. Applied knowledge is power. That is the power to change and the power to learn a better way to behave, instead of staying in the rut of how you were programmed in your family of origins.

Make sure both husband and wife are aware of the financial pressures facing the family. My husband likes to deal with the nuts and bolts, the intricate details of things I don't!

Communication is the most successful approach in getting what you want. It is really important to speak to each other in an "I'm OK, You're OK" tone, body language as well as words. Basically, we are talking about communication that says "I respect me" and "I respect you". The trouble comes when you speak down to someone with words, tone of voice or body language because you are going to tap into that "deep well of not ok feelings" that have been festering since childhood. Parent to child communication is going to reap a defensive reaction most every time.

Nagging, I assume is a parent to child communication which is really saying "I'm OK, You're not OK". Another thing to remember is that you really have no control over another human being. They are going to do what they choose to do and you can not make them do anything. overcoming a grudge is possible when each person expresses to their partner what they are upset about and why it hurt them.

The other partner must listen to be able to understand from their partner's point of view. Then they should paraphrase what their partner said and why it hurt them. Both need to come to an agreement to not do what it was to hurt the other. The key is to let their partner know that they understand why their partner was hurt. Each needs to ask the other for forgiveness.

When you stand before the preacher with this handsome man or beautiful angel you are pledging to love and cherish, you are entering into a three-way covenant with God and your husband or wife. In Ecclesiastes 4:12(b) God says: "A cord of three strands is not quickly torn apart." Your Eternal Father with whom you made this covenant. A Father who created you, knows you, and desires the best for you. He is all might. All power. And is sovereign over all things. Especially marital problems.

Quotes

Here are some quotes to colour your marriage. *When two people are in love there is nothing in all of eternity that will keep them apart. We don't have to leave our marriages to chance. Love works miracles. Life's so much better and sweet when you can get on with your spouse. As I forgive myself, it becomes easier for me to forgive my husband.*

Be patient to persevere and wait for God to heal. Keep in mind that you are both imperfect people. Only the Lord is perfect. Look to God as the source of all you want to see happen in your marriage, and don't worry about how it will happen. It's your responsibility to pray. It's God's job to answer. Leave it in His hands.

"Me" Time

That's right, you ought to have time to yourselves each week to do as you want to do and spend some time reflecting and introspecting so you can learn from life and move more swiftly towards your personal and marriage goals.

Quality One-On-One Time With Your Spouse

This is a must as it helps couples maintain

connectedness, intimacy, empathy, a feeling of security and inner peace. It should be fun and preferably novel, without real world or digital distractions, and can be spent at home, in the park, doing a fun activity, going for a meal, going for a coffee, exploring somewhere new, and so on. Let your imagination help you.

Appreciation

Small, frequent tokens of appreciation are vital and whilst some research suggests that appreciation may be one of the main reasons marriages last a lifetime, common sense would suggest so, too. We can show our genuine appreciation over anything they do for us or bring to our lives, physically or psychologically.

Emotional Intimacy

Spend at least 15-30 minutes daily, connecting emotionally, listening, sharing, supporting, laughing. We rarely have emotional intimacy with anyone the way we do with our spouse so appreciate it and nurture it, daily.

Physical Intimacy

This can be touching, kissing, cuddling, hand holding, frisking, and of course, intimacy in the bedroom. The simple stuff is where to start if you are feeling disconnected and make sure it's frequent. We only have this level of intimacy with our spouse so appreciate that someone wants to be physical with you, understand the importance of it and nurture it.

Prayer Point

- I refuse to sit in any evil seat constructed for me by every enemy of my marriage in Jesus' Name.
- My marriage will not be what the enemy wants it to be in the name of Jesus.
- The name of Jesus shall not fail in my marital case in the name of Jesus.
- When my miracle is coming, I will not annoy God in the name of Jesus.
- I refuse faith-suffocating problems, in my marital case in the name of Jesus.
- I shall be victorious whether in the presence or absence of my enemy in the mighty name of Jesus.
- Every trick and plan of the devil at the edge of my miracle shall not prosper over my life in the name of Jesus.
- Whatsoever that will make me to fail God at the edge of miracle, in the name of Jesus fail woefully.
- Every demonic trap holding my marriage to ransom be destroyed beyond repair in Jesus name.

- You vagabond spirit operating in the life of partner be bound forever in the name of Jesus.
- I bind every spirit of marital fruitlessness in my life and in the life of my partner in the name of Jesus.
- Lord, let the crown of marital success be placed in my head in the name of Jesus.

Value what makes him unique

A man wants to be treated like a king, respected as a man, admired like a hero, and inspired to be all he can be. And when that happens, his wife reaps the benefits!

The respect husbands long for is not based on performance, but rather on their God-given role in the home. Respect from a wife encourages a man and gives him confidence. It can even kindle fresh love in a struggling relationship.

There are men who have highly-destructive habits and a wife's respect naturally diminishes. We can't take sinful behavior lightly, and there are biblical means to deal with these situations.

But in general, all of us are selfish sinners. None of us have perfect track records. I've learned how important mercy, forgiveness and grace play out in every marriage (Ephesians 4:32).

All men and women are made in the image of God (Genesis 1:27), and everyone is uniquely fashioned for God's purposes and delight.

When I take time to recognize my husband's unique creation, I discover characteristics that make him attractive and perfect for me. This is part of the adventure of marriage—discovering and describing what makes our spouse so wonderful, just as Solomon's bride described her "beloved" (Song of Solomon 5:15-16).

Looks can change, so opportunities to admire physical traits may lessen over time (although most men "season" better than women).

But admiration is not just about the way a man looks. We can also see, admire and value worthy attitudes and actions. The way he leads, protects and provides. Record each trait in your mind and heart. Ponder them. Value what makes your husband such a unique "work of art."

Keep Your Focus On God, Not Your Husband's Struggle

Every successful marriage has to have God as the head of their home. Each spouse draws closer to God and to each other as he or she works on an individual relationship with God.

However, if one of them moves the focus away from God, they move back toward their respective corner, farther apart from God and each other.

Expect God to intervene in your husband's struggle. If your husband pulls away from God, stay strong in the Lord and continue praying for him. Prayer can help your husband maintain joy, tranquility, maybe even peace, in the midst of the trial and maybe reap a benefit rather than a penalty.

Carry the problem to God, but don't carry the burden on your shoulders. It's hard not to, but God doesn't want you doing His work.

It's painful to watch our loved one go through hard times, but don't think that your prayers aren't helping. You may not see a breakthrough for a long time, but don't lose hope.

God wants more for your husband than you do, and in the end, if you continue taking everything to God in prayer, God will get the glory for the way He resolves it. Don't stop praying for your husband when the struggle or crisis is over.

Prayer Point:

My father and Lord, in the name of JESUS, you know that my husband is struggling with something that he cannot fix.

You are the Lord of our home and the head of my husband and I ask you in the name of Jesus to take control over our home and let your will rule in our lives.

Thank you God that I can come before you and take whatever is bothering my husband and put it at your feet, fully trusting that your will is done in his life.

Affirmations for achieving forgiveness

1. The door to my heart opens inward

2. I move through forgiveness to love

3. As I change my thoughts, the world around me changes.

4. The past is over, so it has no power now. The thoughts of this moment create my future.

5. It is not fun being a victim.

6. I refuse to be helpless anymore.

7. I claim my own power.

8. I give myself the gift of freedom from past and move with joy into the now.

9. There is no problem too big or too small that it can't be solved with love.

10. I am ready to be healed, I am willing to forgive and all is well.

11. I know that old negative patterns no longer limit me. I let them go with ease.

12. As I forgive myself it becomes easier to forgive others.

13. I forgive myself for not being perfect. I am living

the very best way that I know how

Through the power of the Holy Spirit I have discovered the importance of praying for my husband.

Prayer is a life changing, uninterrupted connection to our heavenly father for his will to be done in our marriage through the power of the Holy spirit.

The power that God has given us as women so that we can honour, respect and serve our husbands with kindness and a pure heart.

Correct use of words. One comment, or one note, can minister healing and uplift him. remember, your encouragement and affirming words will inspire him more than anyone else's. You can send a short email, text a loving thought, or leave an unexpected note.

When we use our words to make our husbands feel small or unimportant, we are damaging him and weakening our bond together.

However when we encourage his dreams rather than squashing them and remind him of his strengths we make our marriage stand stronger.

We both need each other emotionally, physically and spiritually in all aspects. Just as most women desire to be loved above all else, most men desire to be respected above all else. Always remind him that he is respected and respectable.

Proverbs 31:12

I declare and decree, am a noble woman to my husband, I do him good all the days of my life.

I am my husbands best friend

I am grateful to God for his life and being the provider, daddy to our children and friend to us.

I strive to only speak well of him and build him up in front of others no matter what the situation may be

Romans12:18

I decree and declare we live peaceably well with each other

Avoiding Fights

Colossians 3:12-14

Are there battles you pick with your spouse that are avoidable. It could be a rude answer and it all sparks from there. Fire cant put out fire. A soft answer can calm things down. Instead of fighting and arguing with our husbands, ask the Holy Spirit to give you the grace, patience and meekness to understand him.

Nearly all women have a special gift of being naturally soft and tender hearted, inherently empathetic, kind, compassionate and loving.

When we share and pour our time and efforts into

sharing all these God given traits with our families, we are bound to create a more peaceful and loving home.

His Heart, Soul And Mind

When wives take time and energy to focus intently on their husbands spiritual needs, they will begin to see things they might have missed otherwise.

In our fast-paced country, about the only things we focus on are computer screens, cell phones, and TV screens, but a marriage can dramatically improve when we learn to focus on our man.

Heart – when we get married we become one flesh. This bond is created through love. To love him with all my heart means making Him my greatest treasure. Valuing my relationship with my husband ,children and God being our center in life and our the ultimate joy.

Wherever your treasure is, there the desires of your heart will also be. Matthew 6:21

Soul – Your soul is who you are. My soul is who I am. It's the part of me that lives forever. Loving and caring for my husband with all my soul means loving Him with all I am.

Your soul is what integrates, what connects, what binds together your will, then your mind (those thoughts, feelings, and desires going on all the time), and then your body (with all of its appetites, habits, and behavior). ~John Ortberg

Mind –Loving God first with all my mind gives me strategies and ways to handle my marriage in amore positive way God's Word is the ultimate marriage manual. He tells us:

"Be angry, and yet do not sin; do not let the sun go down on your anger, and do not give the devil an opportunity" (Ephesians 4:26-27 NAS).

We marry in the heat of emotions, but a true covenant-marriage develops and grows into a lasting relationship. A relationship that glorifies God, produces healthy children, and most of all, good role models to those people young and old around you.

Praise Him In Private And In Public.

Your husband lives in a world where it's important for him to know that he's winning.Wise wives will look for opportunities to let their husbands know what they are doing well.

I adored my husband during the first precious years of marriage, and I told him always how handsome and cool he is.

But with the passing of time, especially as children came along, I stopped adoring and started pointing out all the wrong I saw in him.

Then one Sunday, a man in one of the events we had gone to attend, called me while talking to him and said to me you are so lucky my dear to have such A man in your life, another one standing beside gushed about my husband's kindness.

During my journey with him I've truly met lots of people speaking great things that praised his motivation, others, his friendly smile. I then glanced over at my husband and knew it was all true and reaffirmed it to him again.

Though I'd never criticized my husband openly to people, God saw my heart. But that day, through others' eyes, I saw my partner as I hadn't seen him in a long time. And I saw how my failure to admire and respect him was not a healthy part of our marriage.

When a wife has true respect in her heart, she is motivated to generate life-giving words of admiration and praise. She will speak well of her husband in private and public.

Prayer Points:

I decree and declare my husband is satisfied and filled with all good things in Jesus Name.

I decree and declare I have a willing heart and mind to honour my husband

Let the angels of God pursue all my pursuers to surrender, in the name of Jesus.

Julian Businge

Chapter 5

Caring For Your Marriage

Julian Businge

Rate Yourself As A Wife

As a wife you need to answer the following sincerely. Answer 'Yes' or 'No'. It will help you to renew your marriage. Be truthful to yourself, it is good for your home.

	Yes	No
1. You have not told him "I love you" for the past one month?		
2. You argue with your husband?		
3. You insulted or cursed him at least once?		
4. You only give him sex when you feel like?		
5. You have not bought a gift for him in the last three months?		
6. You fight regularly about sex?		
7. You engaged in fighting his mother?		
8. You love your family more than his?		
9. You only know how to prepare your local food?		
10. You find it easier to confide in your friends?		

	Yes	No
11. You do nothing to celebrate his last birthday?		
12. You are closer to your mother than him?		
13. You don't enjoy his company?		
14. You have not prayed for him today?		
15. You attend different churches?		
16. You do keep malice with him?		
17. You do not talk to him intimately?		
18. He doesn't know how much you earn?		
19. You wish you are married to someone else?		
20. You do take revenge when he offends you?		
21. You keep secrets from him?		
22. You hate sex?		
23. You love it when he travels?		
24. You don't have him in mind when you are dressing up?		

Breakthrough Declarations

	Yes	No
25. You have not prayed together in the last one week		
26. You do disrespect him when you are angry?		
27. You love your children more than him?		
28. You do report him to friends and family members?		
29. You have not listened to any marriage tapes in the last three months?		
30. You have not invited him for sex in the last six months?		
31. You give him cold sex; no response, no movement?		
32. You respect your pastor more than him?		
33. You've not eaten together in the last one week?		
34. You do feel at home when he is not at home?		
35. You do stop cooking for him when you are angry?		

	Yes	No
36. You've fought him publicly at least once?		
37. You abuse or fought him before visitors and children?		
38. You do not know the size of his shoe?		
39. You've never had bath together?		
40. You don't crack jokes together?		
41. You know you are stubborn?		
42. He is not your hero or mentor?		
43. If you were to remarry you will not marry him?		
44. You have not told him any romantic words in the last one month?		
45. You are not too close?		
46. You don't know the size of his shirt?		
47. He complains about how dirty the house looks like?		
48. You blame him for the state of your marriage?		

Breakthrough Declarations

	Yes	No
49. You don't pray regularly about your marriage; your love and sex life?		
50. You don't respect him?		

Prayer Point

I reject every satanic judgment over my marriage in the name of Jesus.

Father Lord, deliver my spirit and soul from every useless marital journey I have ever undertaken in the name of Jesus.

Every household power working against the fulfillment of the program of God for my marriage, be disgraced and be exposed in the mighty name of Jesus.

Things That Can Make Your Man Stop Loving You

While you may think that you must do something very major in order for your relationship to go sour, the truth is that there are some apparently small things that have major consequences. As a woman, there are some things that you may do without even thinking about them, which may seem very insignificant. Unfortunately, such apparently small things may make the love of your man vanish. Let us take a look at some of the things you should be aware of so that you do not fall victim to a broken relationship.

Making pretense

You try to be something or someone you are not, the man will really hate you for it when he discovers the truth. And the truth eventually shows through. Do not fake interests you do not really have in a bid to attract a man. One of the things that we usually think that we must lie about is our age. But even this may ruin your relationship.

Being dependent

While men would like us to want them, they do not take kindly to the women who seem unable to survive without them. He will simply avoid you as he looks for some breathing space.

Poor listening skills

In general, we often talk more than the men. However, you may get so carried away with your own talking that you do not pay attention to him. Let him tell you about his side as well if you want him to keep on loving you.

Poor spending habits

Once you have gotten closer together, the man may share his money with you. When he notices that you spend money carelessly, he will lose interest in you. You should both make a budget, and ensure that you stick to it.

Thinking of yourself

You should bear in mind that a relationship involves two people. When you constantly think of your own needs, the man's love will wane. Both of you should take part in planning and carrying out the plans.

Playing with his emotions

In case you do not really feel anything special for a man, do not mislead him and drawing his emotions.

Outrunning him

You should take things one step at a time. Do not try to rush him into commitments he is not yet ready for. If you seem to be nagging him, he will lose interest in the relationship.

Being too rigid

When you do not change your mind on some things no matter what, he will change his mind about you instead. And you should not blow things out of proportion.

The 3 Principles By Sydney Banks

The term Three Principles refers to the innate gifts of **Mind, Thought and Consciousness** which every human being uses to generate their experience of life from one moment to the next. These principles provide a universal blueprint for understanding how and why life appears to be the way it is for each of us, and that understanding in itself transforms the way we experience life.

Although the truth underlying these principles has been spoken of by many wise teachers throughout the ages, it was an ordinary working man named Sydney Banks (1931-2009) who, via an extraordinary insight into the nature of his own experience, was able to describe what he had realized in an accessible way that could be grasped by anyone. These principles operate behind the scenes of our everyday experience, and an appreciation of how they function fosters what is commonly called an 'inside-out' understanding of life.

To understand life in this way is to realize that your entire experience of life is being created from within you, despite all appearances to the contrary.

Why is it helpful to learn about the principles?

The principles shine a light on our own true nature, and have enabled many thousands of people worldwide to free themselves from a life of insecurity, struggle, addictive and destructive behaviour patterns, relationship difficulties and a whole spectrum of psychological and emotional problems. These remarkable benefits, and many more besides, occur quite naturally as a result of seeing how these universal faculties are functioning within all of us. The simple realization of the nature of the principles brings forth the innate wisdom, creativity and psychological health that resides within everyone.

As our minds get calmer and clearer, virtually every indicator of human well-being shows an improvement, from self-confidence and communication to resilience and performance at work. Relationships become easier. Physical health improves as we learn to attune to our inbuilt body-wisdom. We stop being so driven by conditioned ideas of what we think we should be doing, ought to do or have to do, and begin to discover and live from what we are truly capable of.

Isn't this the same as mindfulness or similar teachings?

The wisdom teachings throughout the ages have agreed upon one basic fact: what we are looking for is already inside us. Peace of mind, clarity, wisdom, compassion, happiness and fulfillment in life are not to be found by external means, for they are innate human qualities that emerge by themselves when we are in alignment with our essential nature.

Whilst many great teachers have realized this fact for themselves, very few have managed to communicate it to others in such a way that they, too, could have a similarly life-changing realization. As a result, what starts out as a simple, direct and spontaneous insight for one person frequently turns into an increasingly complicated and never-ending series of practices and techniques for everyone else.

The principles, by contrast, continue to be a straightforward and accessible approach that remains refreshingly free of dogma. For those who are struggling in life, they bring the hope and real possibility that sustainable change can occur, no matter how difficult things have been. For those who are already doing well in life, they awaken creativity, increase resilience, unleash hidden potential and bring forth a deeper sense of meaning and purpose in life.

One major difference is that there is no requirement to practice any kind of technique, or to believe in anything in order to experience the benefits of learning these principles. Just like gravity or electricity, these are natural forces that work impartially for everyone - the only variable is our own degree of awareness as to how they operate. The deeper we realize how the principles function within us, the more we experience being in the flow of life. It's that simple.

1. CONSCIOUSNESS

Relationships are meant to be enjoyed! They are meant to be spiritual journeys between two souls and they are meant to be be based in the energy of love.

- **Choose**

Do you want to be in love with your partner or in ego with your partner ? Are you operating from the energy of your heart and soul or the energy of your ego / judging, analysing, doubtful, fearful mind ? Be conscious and focus on what energy you are contributing to your relationship.

- **Point Out**

Everything that you love and appreciate about your partner daily, focus your attention to be in a state of appreciation, Remember, where attention goes, energy flows. If you are consciously making the effort to focus on what you love about them, you will notice more of this and vice versa! If you focus on point out everything that you don't love about your partner, guess what you're going to notice more of ?

- **Be Intuitive**

You are intelligent enough to know your partners soul and who they really are, be observant enough to know when your partner really means what they say, we all say things that we don't mean when we are out of alignment with ourselves / stressed and none of us deserve to be raked over the coals for this, because it just isn't a true representation of our soul. Give them space and let them appologise when they have had time to come back into their alignment.

- **Be Happy**

Take responisibility for your own alignment and inner happiness, no one else can do this for you, expecting your partner to 'Make You Happy' is an almost impossible task and very conditional love. What if two people were to take care of their own alignment and inner happiness and then enjoy each others company in a harmonious, compatible, loving way, adding positively to each others life experience.

- **Create**

What if you were to let go of 'monogamy' and societies expectations? What if you were to really tune in with your soul and discover what is (and what is not) important for you in a relationship and create it to be your own unique experience ? For example I now choose to let go of what a relationship 'should look like' and I create/contribute from a place of what feels enjoyable for my unique experience.

- **Equality**

A lot of the time we expect men and woman to 'play' a certain role in a relationship, yet at a soul level we are all a balance of masculine and feminine energy.

Both deserve to be treated with love, what if you were to take your man on a date and let him feel pampered ? Or other 'role reversal' ideas where you both get to enjoy the best aspects of a relationship, it also helps to understand and appreciate what the other person does for you on a deeper level as well as letting go of expectaions from one another according to gender.

- **Fall in love with yourself too**

Being in a relationship is a great opportunity to not only fall in love with someone else (and vice versa) , but to also fall in love with yourself... Being the most loving, fun, happy, creative, beautiful, sensual and caring person you can be to another person is actually a great way to see your own light, to realize how beautiful you are inside and out. Be the best you that you have to offer and love yourself for it!

Am I being what I am wanting to receive?

Something to be very conscious of is this - If you are wanting a loving and compatible relationship, are you being a loving and compatible componant? If you are expecting someone to love you unconditionally, are you willing to unconditionally love them? Think about what you are 'vibrating out' and what you are attracting back in a relationship.

Learn

Soul Mate relationships are all about co-creative

expansion on a soul level, be conscious to see what is really going on when you feel there is a challenge in your relationship and how you can expand and learn from it as a spiritual being, either internally / individually or as a team, lessons are always blessings in disguise, find your way through 'challenge mode'.

Let them be

Every person is on their own spiritual journey experiencing their consciousness and it is all in perfect timing, let them be, let them follow their own inner guidance as to what they are ready for , don't push or preach, appreciate your own journey and allow others to have theirs, inspire with your living example and if they are ready and interested, they will ask.

2. THOUGHT

Despite the title, no amount of positive thinking can guarantee you a good relationship, but to have a successful relationship you need to think and speak positively about your partner. The need for positive thoughts and words can also be extended to your views about committed relationships, since our opinions about relationships in general affect how we relate to our partner.

If you are not convinced that positive thoughts can make relationships better, hopefully you will at least concede that negative thoughts can poison a relationship. Here are some typical attitudes to avoid if your goal for your relationship is happiness.

The Ball and Chain- I am sure everyone has known a couple that was getting married and one of the pair constantly bemoaned how they will be losing their freedom. You can usually tell more about a person when they're joking than when they're serious. If you feel the constant need to complain about all that you'll be giving up when you're no longer single, then you're not ready to be married.

Over time, the joking turned into real bitterness about feeling tied down by marriage. This is not to say that these people wouldn't have ended up bitter even if they didn't talk so negatively about marriage, but it certainly didn't put them off to a good start.

The Lucky Catch- I've known quite a few men and women that describe themselves as "a great catch." It may be that they make a lot of money or are good looking or both, or it may just be that they perceive themselves this way. For whatever reason they're convinced that their partner was lucky to get a great catch such as themselves. Aside from the ego issues, the problem with thinking that your partner is so lucky is that on the flip side you are implying that you are unlucky.

This is another one of those scenarios that seems to start out innocently enough with one person joking around about how lucky their partner is to have them, but the "innocent" teasing often becomes intentional very quickly.

These relationships seem to end with either the great catch deciding that they should find someone who is a little more worthy of them, or with the other person tiring of being made to feel inferior by always having to hear how lucky they are to have found the great catch.

Support Group or Misery Loves Company?- It's especially important to women to have a support group when times are rough. But, you should feel better, not worse, after you've unloaded your problems on your friends.

Most people agree that when we surround ourselves with positive people that we feel better, and when we spend too much time with negative people we're likely to feel depressed. Many work places have a group of people that commiserate about how awful their jobs are, and once someone starts spending time with that group they also start disliking work. The same is true of relationships. If speaking to a friend about a problem in your relationship results in you having more complaints about your partner at the end of the conversation than you did at the beginning, then this is a misery loves company kind of friend, not a supportive one.

Unless your goal is to feel even more dissatisfied with your relationship, don't discuss your problems with the misery loves company crowd. Obviously, speaking and thinking positively about committed relationships as well as your partner is not a guarantee of happiness. On the other hand, if you think about the happiest couples that you know I'm sure that they all speak very positively about each other and the entire notion of long term relationships.

Not everyone in the scenarios above could have saved their relationships if they had thought and spoken about relationships in a positive way, but it is true that if you say and think something enough times that you start to believe it. If the things that you think and say about commitment and your partner are always negative, then it is bound to have a negative effect on your relationship.

Positive Thoughts, Better Relationships

If your relationships aren't quite what you'd like them to be, you can change that. You don't have to find brand new relationships, although the Law of Attraction can help you with that. You can change the way your relationship is in order to make a better relationship, with the person that you are already with.

- **Focus on good**

Remember that the Law of Attraction is brining good things to yourself by focusing on good and by thinking positive thoughts. If your relationships are suffering for any reason, chances are that there is a lot of negative energy flowing through your relationship, for one reason or another.

The best thing that you can do is begin to focus on the good qualities in the person that you have a relationship with. Try to think about why you were attracted to that person in the first place, and try to focus on the good things about that person. The more that you can focus on those good qualities, the more your partner will be able to display those good qualities.

You will affect your relationship by focusing on the good. For instance, the things that you say to your mate when you are focusing on the good attributes are vastly different than the things that you say when you are caught up in the negative. The more positive things you say to him or her, the more positive behaviors they will exhibit, and the better your relationship will be.

- **Accept them**

Another thing to remember is that in your relationships you should accept the person for who they are. Positive relationships are those that are full of acceptance. If you accept the person that you are with - no matter who they are, this will help you focus on the positive things about them and help you focus on an overall positive relationship.

All in all, positivity is important. The more that you focus on positive thoughts regarding the person you are with, the more that they will be able to reciprocate with positive thoughts on their end. The more positive energy you are able to put into a relationship, the more you will be able to get back from it.

Remember, the Law of Attraction says that what you put out there is what you will get back in time. Therefore, the more positively that you can related to the people you have relationships with, the more positive feelings and thoughts you are going to get back.

Each time you struggle with a relationship, think first about something positive that you can focus on. If your mate is annoying you or exhibiting negative behaviors, see if you can think about something positive - what attracted you to them in the first place. The more that you can focus on the positive, the more positive your relationship will become.

3. MIND

One of the traps in relationships is to understand at least a little the mechanism of the mind that we human beings have developed. To go beyond the repeated robotic program of this ordinary human mind is the beginning of a new possibility for man and woman. For example: the human mind in relationships always seeks to repeat pleasant experiences, sexual or otherwise but this is not intelligent.

It is important for us all to be open to look again fresh at our relationships and at our love making and our lives. One should always be in search of the new.

How many times have you heard someone say," Oh they are boring?" People do not want to be boring; in fact everybody thinks it is the other person who is boring.

The truth is we can all be boring if we do not seek out new ways to change, challenge and live our lives. Change is one of the keys to keeping the love alive and well. Change is everything. This very desire to change will be the galvanising force in recreating a new relationship, once again fresh, alive, vital and happy. This very search will renew us and renew our relationships; we will understand that we are in the relationship together and we can try new things together.

If we have some beautiful experience today, we need not ask for it again tomorrow because now it is meaningless -- we have known it and it is finished. There is no point comparing our experiences as life keeps flowing. Once our relationships have the qualify of exploration and playfulness then love can be re-introduced as each partner acknowledges that it is their responsibility also to keep love alive. This way each party can bring his or her own insight into the relationship to restore the lost vitality, enthusiasm and love.

Overview of these three principles

- Mind is the universal intelligence behind life
- Consciousness creates an awareness of what we call reality
- Thought is the power to create our moment to moment existence

Simply, developing an understanding of these principles is literally life-changing and life-transforming – lifelong 'issues' could drop away, for example, or you could have feelings of invicibility, or life might just be 'nicer'. But the true extent of what this understanding can do for you has to be experienced.

Imagine always knowing where to look for answers, being okay being wrong, being okay with all your experiences of life? Can you imagine taking 100% responsibility for your life, even? Well, all that is available for you, right now – one thought away – via you and your understanding of the 3 principles of mind, consciousness and thought.

Whatever is going on for you! Whether it's relationship issues, or it's health concerns, or it's money worries, or you're simply wanting peace of mind… and all helped by 3 simple steps.

Here Are The Three Steps

- Take your thinking less seriously (take things less personally)

- Results: You have more peace of mind, you worry less, and you get to feel more comfortable in your own skin (Principle of Thought)
- Become more aware of differing possibilities (increase awareness)
- Results: You have more perspective, you get stuck less, and you have more insights and breakthrough (Principle of Consciousness)
- Allow inspiration and new insights to be your guide (access wisdom)
- Results: You start to trust more, you fear less, and you get to live a more inspired and creative life (Principle of Mind).

This is important: understanding the 3 principles is not about understanding the words used to describe them! It matters not whether you or I can explain to others what the 3 principles mean, or even why they're important. It's ALL about the feeling, always.

And when you start to realise just how your life is unfolding, start to take responsibility for your experiences of it, something rather magical happens, it truly does. But this is magic that cannot be explained; it is magic you have to experience for yourself. This magic goes by another name, naturally, and that name is love. But love is just a word, too the experience of it is everything!

Quotes by Sydney Banks

"Your thoughts are like the artist's brush. They create a personal picture of the reality you live in."

— Sydney Banks

"The sickness of the mind are feelings that we create and put onto objects. But if you see the objects without the feelings, then you are healthy."

– Sydney Banks

"If the only thing people learned was not to be afraid of their experience, that alone would change the world." — Sydney Banks

I hope these three principles will help you have a healthier relationship! Power to see and discern, come upon you, in the name of Jesus. Power to over-come, fall upon you now, in the name of Jesus.

Togetherness

Mutuality is one of the most important aspects of marriage success. But how do you become part of a couple while maintaining a strong sense of yourself? How do you manage your need for time together and time apart? And what do you do if you and your partner have different ideas of how much time to spend together?

How much time together is enough? Is there such a thing as too much togetherness? Is there a way to maintain closeness even when your work life is especially demanding of your time and attention, perhaps including prolonged separations? Obviously, these are questions without simple answers, but research on successful marriage indicates that one key is to find the middle ground. According to

David Olsen, couples who are neither too separate from one another, nor overly involved with one another are in the best position to succeed.

Moderate levels of closeness are optimal. Very low or high levels of autonomy in marriage work less well. By the way, the same model applies to your relationships with your families of origin--being neither too close, nor overly distant works best. In fact, we learn our patterns of togetherness and individuality in our families of origin. Different families have different styles. Some families emphasize closeness, while others accentuate individual needs and activities. Your partner will have different expectations shaped by their family experience, so you may have to find a new balance.

It's common for couples to struggle over finding the "right" balance of time spent together and apart, as well as what level of closeness to maintain with one's original family. However, your aim should be to find a cooperative rather than adversarial way to engage in this essential process. Couples may find it challenges them both personally to make changes in style as they both steer for the middle ground by moderating extreme togetherness or autonomy. This is true whether you are both from similar positions on the closeness 'scale' or from different ends of the scale. It's definitely worth the effort to find a path that works for both of you as a couple and for each individually, though.

One important aspect of individuality involves

relationships outside of your marriage. Women are more inclined to rely on friends or relatives, in addition to their partner, for emotional support. Men, on the other hand, tend to rely more on their partner for most of their support. So women sometimes run the risk that their partner may be upset by their degree of involvement with 'outsiders.'

Men may not have sufficient outside support during periods when their partner is less emotionally available. Social patterns that worked well for you previously may shift after marriage to take account of new needs. For example, one person was accustomed to going out on Friday nights out with co-workers to unwind, but their partner wanted to spend Friday evenings together. You may need more time for couples friends in your social schedule after marriage, but will still want to maintain relationships with single friends. Discuss social adjustments with your partner to work out a balance that's comfortable for both of you.

For most couples these days the challenge is finding ways to stay close enough in the face of work and other demands. Researchers like John Gottman tell us that successful couples spend a minimum of 12 to 15 hours of non-sleep, non-TV time together each week. Daily non-stress communication (even just 10 minutes) to keep in touch with each other's lives and other daily bonding rituals also promotes your sense of togetherness.

When you're apart, whether just for a portion of the

day or for extended business travel, how you keep in touch and how you get back together can be more important that how much time you are separated. Successful couples touch base with each other at least once or twice a day, even if for just a few minutes. They also make sure that their reunion receives some attention. Make the time and effort to renew your bond at the end of the day and at the end of the week. Develop familiar rituals that you both enjoy for reconnecting. These can be as simple as trading neck massages or enjoying a cocktail together before the TV comes on.

Couples who use these reconnecting strategies can tolerate more separation while still remaining close to each other. Couples who don't reconnect can feel isolated from each other, even with less separation. In other words, it's not necessarily how much you are separated, but how you manage keeping in touch and renewing your bond.

Lord, let the crown of marital success be placed in my head in the name of Jesus.

The 5 Love Languages by Gary Chapman

Personalize these prayers by replacing the parts of the prayers with your name and that of your spouse where applicable. After making these prayers, believe that God has answered and consolidate your victory by thanking God for the changes you hoped to see and the restoration of your marriage.

The 5 Love Languages are ways to express or receive **love.** How do I express love to others? What do I complain about the most? What do I request most often? Here are the 5 languages that tell the story of love.

Verbal affirmations

According to Dr. Gary Chapman, this language uses words to affirm your partner. The language of love that is spoken can be more powerful than actions and many times has a longer lasting effect. Speaking words to another such as unsolicited compliments hold a great deal of meaning to your partner. On the other hand, insults can shatter a relationship and often leave a lasting impression.

Spending time together

This language is all about giving the other person your undivided attention. If you want to tell someone you love them you can do so by your wiliness and desire to spend quality time with them. Giving someone you undivided attention demonstrates the importance they hold in your life and in your priorities. When you are constantly distracted, miss commitments to spend time together or postpone activities frequently you communicate to the other person that they fall far down on your list of importance.

Giving gifts

Giving gifts should never be substituted for other expressions of love or to make up for a lack of them. Gift giving is not about materialism but rather thoughtfulness. When you pay attention to someone's needs in the form of thoughtful and unexpected gift giving you are showing them that they are important to you. Everyday gestures count the most when communicating love but the occasional gift enhances your expression of love.

Helping hand

Pitching in with everyday chores without being asked or forced is an expression that you care about the other person's time and efforts and want to be a partner in the relationship. Sometimes these are called acts of service and your willingness to provide help with everyday chores shows that you care about the other person.

The language of touch

The language of touch is not about what happens in

the bedroom. Rather, physical touch is used to communicate excitement, concern, care and love. These are hugs, pats on the back, holding hands and other thoughtful touches on the face, arm shoulder, knee, etc. While these physical gestures can show love and concern the opposite can be said about people who physically inaccessible. Being adverse to touch demonstrates an attitude that is neglectful or abusive.

Love Language is all of the thoughtful ways that we can combine to show and reinforce our feelings of love, caring and affection for our partners. People who are aware of the different ways to express their love and practice them will find that they develop a much deeper and meaningful relationship. Obviously it is best that both people in the relationship work at learning how to use the 5 love languages. It leads to a rewarding and more fulfilling relationship for you both.

If you would like your lover to learn to speak the languages of love, print out and have them read this article. It might just lead to you developing your own special language of love. It would be great if you could know exactly which one is your dominant, and could be able to act with people you love accordingly, every time you speak to them? To know for sure whether you are someone who needs to give

What happens to love after the wedding? After the first or second year of marriage, when the initial "tingle" is starting to fade, many couples find that their "love tanks" are empty. They may have been expressing love for their spouse, but in reality they may have been speaking a different love language.

Chapman says, "We're not talking comfort. We're talking love. Love is something we do for someone else. So often couples love one another but they aren't connecting. They are sincere, but sincerity isn't enough."

Challenge if your feeling that your love is fading away. Ask your partner, If, on a scale from zero to ten, it is less than 10, then ask "What can I do to help fill our love for each other?" You will not intervene in the affairs of man by forcing him to go against his own will. Neither can we control the behaviour of another person.

What God does is to bring a change of heart and mind. And what we can do is pray to God and ask Him to touch the heart and mind of our spouse. God will go to places we cannot, and do things that we can only dream of. Use these prayers as guidelines for how to pray for the resolution of all that ills your marriage.

Prayer Point

Heavenly father God, I thank you for who you are and for the promises that you have made concerning me and my spouse. Your Word is ever true and your promise of blessings and multiplication that you have promised me throughout the ages (Genesis 22:17; Hebrews 6:14) is forever mine, in Jesus name.

You have promised to bless me exceedingly and it is your heart's desire to enlarge my coast. Every satanic covenant that is going against your continual and uninterrupted blessing in this marriage, I command it out by the Holy Ghost rain of fire to consume them, in Jesus name.

Give us the strength to work through our differences.

Lord, thank you for the good work that you have started in my marriage. I know that you will do mite to the end. I ask for the strength to stay courageous and strong in your promises as you work out things in our marriage.

Replace every negative feeling with love and help us to work through our differences.

Every man or woman determined to scatter thus marriage will not succeed. Their evil plans will scatter in Jesus name.

I refuse to be tempted to try other alternatives. I will not be discouraged even if it seems that nothing is happening at the moment.

Julian Businge

Chapter 6

Steps to Saving Your Marriage

Julian Businge

Steps to saving your marriage

Are you wondering what you can do to save the relationship? How do you start repairing the damage which has been done?

Every marriage is going to hit a rough patch every now and then. Nothing is ever as good as it is when it first begins, but if your marriage is having problems, there are ways to save the relationship. After all, you still care for each other, but you may have begun putting your marriage on autopilot without even realizing it. Unfortunately, a marriage is something that must be given continuous attention, but it is never too late to turn back the clock.

Find the real issue

There are several different types of arguments and fights which take place in a marriage. Some of those fights happen on a regular basis, but there are others based on petty disagreements. However, it is the arguments which are based on emotions which bring out the real issues in a marriage. Once you have identified the real issues within your marriage you will have a better idea on how to save the relationship.

Are there any outside barriers?

Are there outside influences which are causing disagreements between the two of you? For example, there may be a mother-in-law who is always putting down your spouse or there are work issues which are beginning to drive the two of you apart. If you find problems outside the marriage, think of ways that you can get around these issues and fix them.

No show, no tell

It is not uncommon for couples to put their relationship on auto-pilot if they have been together for a while. However, this is not a way to save the relationship. But many couples still find themselves not saying "I love you" to each other as much anymore or otherwise showing affection.On the other hand, "I love you " may get said, but it lacks the emotion behind it that it used to. This is not because you love any other any less, but rather that you have grown too comfortable.

The good news is this issue is one of the easiest to fix to save the relationship. Simply do something that you know your spouse will appreciate to show them how much you do care for them.

Get back in touch

Life is busy and once you settle into a routine, it is easy for a marriage to become relaxed and lazy. Instead, you will need to spend some time with each other in order to reconnect. Go out for a nice dinner or have a weekend away where it is just the two of you in order to make each other a priority.

Prayer Point:

- I decree and declare that the weapons of my warfare are not carnal, but mighty through God to pull down strongholds, cast down vain imaginations and every high thing that lifts itself against the knowledge of Jesus Christ.

- I establish divine parameters, boundaries, borders, and laws of the kingdom of heaven to govern all activities within my marriage. (1 Chronicles 4:10).

- I overrule, disallow and veto every diabolical sanction, subverting activity, injunction, directive, mandate, or order which opposes the will of the Lord concerning my life, marriage and family (Matthew 18:18).

- Every master spirits seen or unseen,I disarm you and paralyse you.I call on Michael, archangels, and the armies of Heaven to handle all satanic contentions, disputes, strivings, and resistance against God"s plans in my marriage. (Daniel 3:24-25, Hebrews 1:14, Psalm 91:11).

- We are liberated from generational, satanic, demonic alliances, allegiances, soul-ties, spirits of inheritance and curses. I sever them by the sword of the Lord, the blood of Jesus and the power of the Holy Spirit.

- I decree and declare that all invisible and invincible walls in my mind and environment fighting my marriage be destroyed (Colossians 1:16, Joshua 6:1).

- Every power standing between our miracles and breakthroughs, die, in the name of Jesus.

- Troublers of my Israel in the dream, my God shall trouble you today, in the name of Jesus.

- Magnetic curses, family curses, break, in the name of Jesus.

10 Inevitable Things In Marriage

Everyone you marry has a weakness

Only God has no weakness. Every rose flower has its own thorn. If you focus too much on your spouse's weakness, you can't get the best out of his/her strength.

Everyone you marry has a dark history

No one is an angel. Therefore avoid digging into one's past. What matters is the present life of your partner. Old things are passed away. Try to forgive and forget. The past can't be changed. So focus on the present and the future!

Every marriage has its own challenges

Marriage is not a bed of roses. Every shining marriage has gone through its own test of hot and excruciating fire. True love is proved in time of challenge. Fight for your marriage! Make up your mind to stay with your spouse in time of needs. Remember this is the vow you made on your wedding day!

Every marriage has different levels of success

Don't compare your marriage with anyone! We can never be equal, some will be far in front and others far behind. To avoid marriage stresses, be patient, work hard and with time, your marriage dreams shall come true.

To marry is to declare a war

When you marry, you must declare a war against enemies of marriage. Some of the enemies of marriage are:

- Ignorance
- Rumors
- Prayerlessness
- Unforgiveness
- Adultery
- Third Party Influence
- Stinginess
- Stubbornness
- Lack Of Love
- Rudeness
- Wife battery
- Laziness
- Winning
- Nagging
- PRIDE
- Divorce.
- Etc.

Be ready to fight to maintain your marriage zone.

There is no perfect marriage

There is no ready made marriage anywhere. Marriage is hard work, volunteer yourself and perfect it daily. Marriage is like a **motor car** with a gear oil, gear box, etc. If these parts are not properly maintained, the car will break down somewhere along the road and expose the occupant to unhealthy circumstances. Many people are careless about our marriage. What about you? If you are, please pay attention to your marriage.

God cannot give you the complete person you desire

God gives you your partner in form of raw materials in order for you to mold what you desire. You may desire a woman who can pray for 1 hour but your wife can only pray for 30 minutes. With your love, prayer and encouragement, she can improve.

To marry is to take a risk

You cannot predict what will happen after marriage, as situations change. So, leave a room for adjustment. Pregnancy may not come in the next 4 years. You may get married to her because she's slim but she becomes a little fat after a child. Your husband may lose his beautiful job for years that you have to take the financial responsibility of the family until he gets a new job. But with God by your side, you will smile at long last.

Marriage is not a contract, it is permanent

"Whosoever putteth away his wife, and marrieth another, committeth adultery: and whosoever marrieth her that is put away from her husband committeth adultery" (Luke 16: 18). Marriage needs total commitment. Love is the glue that makes a couple stick together. Divorce starts in the mind. Never think of divorce! Never threaten your spouse with divorce. Choose to remain married! God hates divorce, though it's permitted only in extreme cases.

Every marriage has a price to pay

Marriage is like a bank account. It is the money you deposit into your bank account that you can withdraw. If you don't deposit love, peace and care into your marriage, you are not a candidate of a blissful home. There is no free love in marriage, You cannot love without giving and sacrificing.

Prayer Point:

- Lord, I thank you because; marriage and staying married is your will for me. God of mercies, give me the grace and mercy to grow old together with my husband and forgive our sins in Jesus' name.

- There shall be peace in my marriage in Jesus' name.

- You pursuer of my marriage, be pursued by angels of God, in the name of Jesus.

- I stand against prayer paralysis in my family by the blood of Jesus.

- I command blindness to fall on every stubborn pursuer of my marriage, in the name of Jesus.

- Every cause of torment by wicked intelligent network in my family, be nullified by the blood of Jesus.

Don't blame your partner for everything

Blame can be a really toxic thing in relationships. Being on the receiving end of blame can be exhausting, exasperating, and painful. It can make you feel tiny: like nothing you do is good enough or ever will be. It can break down your sense of trust in your partner and replace it with a growing sense of resentment and anger. And, if it persists for a very long time, constant blame in a relationship can be a symptom of emotional abuse. We often think of blame as being something we do when we're trying to attack someone or make them feel bad - and, in some cases, this is definitely true.

But blame can also be a defensive thing. It can be something we do when we feel we aren't being noticed or cared for in the way that we would want to be. And, even more commonly, it can also be something we do because we are struggling to understand or deal with our own emotions - preferring instead to project them onto other people.

A woman who tells her partner: 'You never listen to me' may be expressing themselves critically, but, in another sense, they are also communicating something: that they want to be heard. Likewise, a man who tells his partner, 'You don't have any respect for me' is perhaps exaggerating, or even choosing to ignore the times that his partner has shown their respect, but, again, is also expressing something else - a need that they feel isn't being met.

This isn't to excuse blame - clearly, this isn't a productive way to express feelings and it can have negative consequences on the couple relationship - but rather to contextualise it, and give some indication as to why we so often turn to it. Blame is actually one of - if not the - most common features of miscommunication in relationships, because it's very often the instinctive response when we're struggling to face up to our feelings - so many of us do this!

Prayer point:

"God help me to see my husband as You see him."

- Lord Jesus rent your heavens and deliver us from our weaknesses, help and teach us to be transformed and renewed in our minds.
- Let the good testimonies of my marriage come forth in Jesus' name.
- Let the habitation of witches causing us to fight be desolate by the Holy Ghost fire in the name of Jesus.
- Any spirit or power manipulating our dreams die in Jesus' name.
- Every cause of inability to enjoy divine benefits in my life, be nullified by the blood of Jesus, in the name of Jesus.
- Every problem attempting to suffocate my faith, be uprooted by the blood of Jesus.

Make your husband love you forever

At the time of marriage, most women will wish for a husband that can love and take care of them for the rest of their lives. Unfortunately, many wives do not know how to maintain a good marriage.

Every couple will go through the sweetest period of the beginning and slowly give way or slack when things are working in a monotonous manner. Yes, you got your man to fall in love with you, but knowing how to keep your husband in love with you endlessly is another piece of knowledge to learn.

There are many things that you can do to make your husband love you forever. If you want to keep your husband in love with you, you have to make sure the romance and passion should never go off, no matter how long both of you are together. Remember, keeping romance is not only the men's job, but also women.

It may sound very shallow that most guys wish for their wives to be best. To be honest, who doesn't like good stuffs, right? Men love women who are always improving. It is actually one of the ways on how to keep your husband in love with you. You need to be smart and confident, but on the other hand, you also need to act "dumb" sometimes. The reason being because your husband will love even more when he feels his role in your life is important when you seek for his assistance and advices sometimes. Men as much as women like their wives to adore them.

Prayer Point

- Every household evil traders trading with my marriage be bound and be roasted by fire.No evil will come near our dwelling
- Every arm of evil re-enforcement in my marriage be a scattered by fire of God and be roasted in Jesus' name.
- I refuse, frustrate and destroy enemy re-establishment of my evil covenants in marriage.
- I decree enough is enough of my unprofitable fights and querrals in my marriage.I speak unity and peace in my home.
- I destroy all my evil monitoring gadgets on my marriage.
- Let my wasters and my delayers in marriage be found no more after the order of Pharaoh.
- I declare my ways open to victory in Jesus' name.
- I refuse to cry in vain over my marriage in Jesus name.
- Every cause of suffering from marital attacks, be nullified by the blood of Jesus.

Julian Businge

Chapter 7

Praying For Your Marriage

Julian Businge

.

Affirmations for a strong and loving relationship

People who "fall out of love" don't just stop loving each other overnight. It starts because they get comfortable and eventually, take one another for granted. I am sure you don't ever want to look at your husband and wonder who he is or why you're together.

I want the love and the bond you have for each other to last a lifetime. But, I want to let you know that it's going to take unconditional love, prayer, and a powerful commitment to make it happen.

In this chapter, you will learn some powerful affirmations to rekindle your marriage and love.

Here we go…

- My marriage is prayerful, powerful, and passionate.
- My marriage is a joy and a gift from God.
- I am loyal, devoted, and compassionate every day to my partner.
- My partner is one of my greatest blessings, and I will treat him with honor and respect.
- My partner is capable of becoming the person God created him to be.
- We strive for greatness in our marriage and will not settle for anything less.

- I enjoy falling in love with the same person over and over again as if for the first time.
- My marriage is free from hurt, anger, and lack.
- My marriage is full of abundance, love, and compassion.
- I accept responsibility for my actions and make right my wrongs.
- I feel safe and protected by my partner.
- I look at my partner through my eyes via my heart.
- I have a twinkle in my eye for my partner.
- I put my best foot forward in my marriage.
- No one is perfect, including me.
- I am understanding.
- My goal is always to create harmony and clarity.
- I listen to understand and not to "win."
- No one ever wins in an argument.
- I communicate in peace and with compassion.
- I remain in balance with my emotions.
- I practice patience with grace and ease.
- I am flexible.
- I create the foundation on which my relationship is built.

Practice these everyday, and it shall be well with you in Jesus name.

Prayer for a strong marriage bond

Father, life gets so busy and things can creep into our marriage and cause distance. Help us be intentional in spending time together and reveal things that are creating a chasm in our relationship. Protect us from things that will divide us, whether it be time spent online or a recreational activity or a friendship that is taking away from our marriage. Help us know how to remedy the situation and bring a closeness back into our marriage with You at the center. I pray these things with complete confidence in Jesus and Your Spirit at work in our marriage. Amen.

Let God be God in my marriage
I suggest that you take a Psalm 126 as your Scripture Reading and Psalm 124:8 for Confession.

- Angels of God pick all my marital breakthroughs and blessings in the "go-slow" of life and bring them to us speedly by fire in the name of Jesus.
- Lord, give me the keys of divine breakthrough in Jesus name. The oil well in my glorious marital treasure shall not dry in the name of Jesus.
- I receive power to become a beneficiary of divine marital assistance during this program in the name of Jesus.
- My miracle shall not disappear with this month in the name of Jesus.

Lord, append your stamp of restoration in my marriage in the name of Jesus.

- Father Lord, stamp out all the undesirable things in my life in the name of Jesus.

- Lord, set an edge over my mouth that I may not say anything unpleasant to You in the name of Jesus.

- Lord, pound me and make me into the shape you   want.
Lord breath into every part of my being in the name of Jesus.

- Lord, let the fruits of prayer grow and manifest in me in the name of Jesus.

- Any power that is not interested in joy in our home I command you to fall down and die in the name of Jesus.

- Every seat of witchcraft in my family/ marriage / house be unseated by fire in the name of Jesus.

- Let every path-way of witchcraft into my life be overturned by the blood of Jesus in the name of Jesus.

- Every stubborn cause of failure in my life I bury and destroyed you by fire in the name of Jesus.

- Any member of my family empowering external enemies, die by thunder in the name of Jesus.

- You family foundational bondage affecting and disgracing my life, I terminate and destroy your activities by the blood of Jesus in the name of Jesus.

Prayer against divorce or separation

Do you feel like your relationship is in trouble? Perhaps your better half has left, your marriage is on the rocks, or you simply feel out of place with the person you are with. You value the relationship that you have with your husband or wife, and you honour and respect the vows that you took in front of God and witnesses.

Despite the best of intentions, there are times when even the most perfect relationship has problems and issues. It is common for a member of the relationship to run-away from those problems, or refuse to face them by trying to leave the relationship and the home you've made together. Do not despair, there is hope, you just have to find faith and encouragement from our most gracious Lord and saviour Jesus.

Prayer can repair the most damaged marriage. The power of God can bring two people, who are intended to be together, back into a love filled marriage. Your union will know the love from the blessings of God if you keep your eyes on Him in all things. Through prayer, anything is possible. God is all-powerful and all-knowing. He can mend any bridges that may have been burned by conflict, clear away any confusion, and give you the power to forgive when needed most. If your relationship is in need of a blessing and you have nowhere to turn, always consider the power of prayer. God is always there to listen, and his followers on earth are always ready to assist in having your prayer requests heard.

My father in heaven, I run to you for you are my refuge ,I need Your help and closeness. You are my ever present helper in time of need. Please make changes in my spouse's heart.

Change me too Lord by your spirit where I have failed , Make us compatible again, and bring us closer together as we were before. Fill us with Your love and give us the strength to love one another, care for one another.

Let your presence make us new creatures free from all the harm caused by careless, uncalled for words, and the pain caused by emotional distance.

Prayer Point

Heal the division between the two of us. Make us one again. In Your precious name I pray, amen. **MARRIAGE KILLERS** be destroyed in Jesus' name:

- Oh Lord, thou art the most righteous judge let the divorce suit filed by my husband be handled by the Holy Ghost for your word says you hate divorce in Jesus' name.
- Father Lord, I refuse to be separated from my husband in the name of Jesus.
- Father Lord, fault all the excuses advanced by my husband to advance Your favor upon my life in Jesus mighty name.
- I withdraw the divorce suit from the hands of satanic agents unto the hand of the Holy Spirit in the name of Jesus.
- Father Lord depose every human agent of the enemy appointed to put asunder my marriage in Jesus' name.
- Rock of ages, let Your hammer break into pieces all the seats arranged by the devil for the judgment against my marriage.

- Father Lord, reverse the divorce suit into a new wedding with my husband in Jesus name.
- Father Lord, let all the powers supporting the separation be devoured by the Lion of Judah in Jesus' name.
- All territorial weapons fashioned against my marital life will not prosper in Jesus name.
- I refuse to answer anymore satanic calling of my name in Jesus' name.

Prayer for money management in marriage

My precious Lord. Please help us to rely on You more in our marriage when it comes to our finances.

May Your Holy Spirit fill us with wisdom in how to manage our finances, give us generous hearts to give to those in need, and teach us to not worry about money so much.

We pray there would be peace in our marriage, especially over finances, at all times, and in all ways. May Your presence keep us grounded, keep us calm, and keep us in Your will always.

Prayer Point

God Almighty give us both wisdom and understanding for how to handle financial responsibilities. May we be thoughtful as we work together to create a budget, pay off bills, and spend for needs let there be divine alignment on Gods kingdom principles that we may be able to prosper.

Any areas where we disagree about spending or saving money, our God give us clarity and agreement. In Jesus' name Amen.

- All my hidden marital blessing in the second heaven come out by fire in the name of Jesus.
- I pray against every spirit of lack and poverty. Oh Lord, let your blessing that makes us rich fall on us and all generations to come saturate this marriage in Jesus' name.
- I lock myself inside the will of God for marriage in the name of Jesus.
- Every satanic attack on my marriage, I paralyze you now in the name of Jesus.
- Every spiritual thief stealing from my divine treasure, fall down and die in the name of Jesus.

- Any spiritual thief stealing away love from my marriage restore it back in Jesus name.
- Heavenly treasurers sign out my divine possession now in the name of Jesus.
- Every wall of partition between me and ——————(name of your spouse) be pulled down in the name of Jesus.
- All the hatred of my in-laws against me, Lord, turn them to love in the name of Jesus.
- Every satanic prophecy presently manifesting in my marriage die with your sender in the name of Jesus.
- Let the fire of God consume every evil wilderness of marriage destruction before me in the name of Jesus.
- Anything in my life that is fertilizing any problem in my marriage receive the destruction of God in Jesus name.
- All the stubborn and difficult areas of my marriage receive divine solution in the name of Jesus.
- Let the river of marital problems in my life dry up now in the name of Jesus.
- O Lord, let me be one of the children that You are going to answer and restore his/her marriage this month in the name of Jesus.
- Begin to thank God for his miracles and begin to see your testimonies and miracles coming to you from hence forth in the name of Jesus.

Prayer for clear communication

Lord, I feel like my partner and I have had a difficult time clearly communicating with one another lately. We are both lacking in our compassion and understanding towards each other.

I pray we would be better than this, and that You will open our hearts to You. Holy Spirit, please help us be better communicators with each other.

I pray that we would live with understanding for what the other person is going through, and that we are thoughtful in our words and actions. Amen.

If your husband doesn't know what their strengths are, pray for them that they will gain clarity and seek to encourage them in those strengths.

Prayer for our strengths

Father we thank you for all the talents, skills and gifts you have given unto us. We pray that we will not be proud about areas of strength in us, but that you would bless others by being great stewards of our gifts and talents faithfully. In Jesus' name Amen

Prayer for any big decisions we havecoming up

Our father and friend we ask you in Jesus name to fill us with divine wisdom regarding this prospective new job, moving, parenting choices or caretaking responsibilities—any decisions we have to make in the future, we lay them at God's feet.

We Ask you God to reveal any red flags or reasons we shouldn't move forward. Give us peace and joy about our decision together as a couple to know that you are with us. In Jesus' name Amen.

Pray for our dreams

Heavenly father God, thank you for all our hearts desires. It is written that if we delight in you, you will give us the desires of our hearts. Therefore today we bring you all our intentions; the ones we never shared, the ones that we have shared together with my spouse.

We surrender those dreams to you God. We Ask you to give us clarity and peace about our dreams. We ask God for patience as we wait for our dreams, and peace for the dreams that must change or be set aside for a while. We give thanks for those already manifesting in us. In Jesus' name. Amen

- I command every evil architect of hatred, hostility, and conflict in my marriage be paralyzed in Jesus' name.
- Oh Lord, arise and disgrace every power challenging my marriage in Jesus name.
- Let all hatred and negative words receive fire of the Holy Ghost in Jesus' name.
- Let all those despising me in my husband's house receive divine disgrace today in Jesus.

- I command all evil transportation systems assigned against my family to halt and be destroyed in Jesus Name
- I command the territorial spirits controlling me from my place of birth to release me in Jesus' name.
- Father Lord, let your fire be kindled against every shrine in my town working against my life and family in Jesus name.

Practical ways to bless your husband

This may be the most unnoticeable one of all of these. But, do you know the power of prayer? This little tool moves mountains and parts seas. Praying for your husband has the ability to, first, soften your heart toward him, then his heart toward you. Prayer can protect him from harm, open doors to spiritual growth and pave the way for him to walk in right paths.

Listen

Personally, I don't like feeling like I am to competing with an i-phone for someone's attention. So, when my husband is speaking, I try to stop what I am doing and fully focus on him. People feel most loved when they feel like they are being listened to.

Speak kind words

I had to memorize this verse to help me stay intentional about the way I speak to people. "She speaks with wisdom, and faithful instruction is on her tongue." Proverbs 31:26

Since men like having their work recognized, easy way to let him hear me speak kind words, is to thank him for the way he provides for us. I also tell him, "thank you for loving me", because honestly, I'm not always the cuddliest cactus to love on. Thank your man for something he did today.

Clean It Up

The house, yes. But more importantly, yourself. I have learned that I am better prepared to minister kindly and graciously to my husband when I like the way I look or feel. This can be achieved by simply touching up my hair, washing my face, putting on a clean shirt, or adding an accessory somewhere. Letting your husband see you in your sweats is okay, too, if he doesn't mind. This effort is more about preparing yourself mentally and physically, than it is about looking good for your husband. We often act the way we feel.

Make this confession loud and clear:

I rise above adversity and I attain new heights of achievement by the power of God. The Almighty God is turning my tribulations into triumphs, failures into fortunes, set backs into successes, obstacles into opportunities, burdens into blessings, I refuse to be hampered by handicaps, I refuse to be dismayed by discouragement.

I refuse to be overcome by opponents, I refuse to be defeated by disappointments, I refuse to be destroyed by disasters. I take divine insurance over disasters, tragedies, physical and spiritual accidents, injuries, infirmities, and distresses, in the name of Jesus.

Prayer Point

Jesus, our intercessor, inspire us to pray without ceasing until something good happens.

Heavenly Father, You have promised that a wife is a good gift from you. I want to be an excellent wife to my husband, one who consistently brings him honour (Proverbs 18:22).

Lead me, Lord, to recognize the ungodliness hiding in my will, my expectations, and how I express my emotions. I want to surrender them to You for healing. Show me where I am investing my attention in things that will deteriorate my relationship with my husband

Let the power of Your Word transform my motives. Coach me relentlessly to be a wife who respects her husband in word and deed. Cause Your tenderness, gentleness, kindness, and humility to become my own (Colossians 3:12).

I want to be a content wife who does not harass my husband with quarrels and fretfulness. Please use me to create a peaceful home for him. Use me to encourage him, bear his burdens, and reflect Your extravagant love for him (Hebrews 13:5 and

Philippians 4:11–12).

I pray these things with complete confidence in Jesus and Your Spirit at work in our marriage. Amen.

Chapter 8

Praying For Your Children

Julian Businge

How To Pray For Your Children

Be in the habit of regularly praying for your kids. Not only does prayer work and change your child, but it also helps you as a parent align yourself with God and his plan. With his strength you willl be less likely to blow up in anger and you will have more wisdom for dealing with life's challenges. Each day, pray that God will give you the strength to maintain your personal control as you work with your children. It's tempting to blow up in anger or give in to constant nagging.

Parenting requires continual perseverance and strength. God provides spiritual resources when emotional resources seem scarce. Learning to trust in him and pray every day for strength will go a long way to provide you with the ability to face the challenges of parenting. Also, pray that God will change your child's heart. It's important to note that nowhere in the Bible does it say that parents change children's hearts. We do read that people can change their own hearts. God calls that repentance. We also see that God changes people's hearts directly.

Ezekiel 36:26 reveals this promise, "I will give you a new heart and put a new spirit in you; I will remove from you your heart of stone and give you a heart of flesh." That's the prayer we want to have for our children every day. Of course, God does use parents to be the instruments to motivate children to change their hearts, so your prayer will be one that allows you to partner directly with God in the changing of the heart of your child. You will also want to pray for relational connection opportunities in the course of your day. After all, much of the business of family life is that you be firm with your children. That toughness often wears at the relationship and so times of connection are important. Remember that children can only take as much pressure as the relationship allows.

Ask the Lord to provide some fun times in your day or a meaningful conversation or a moment where you and your child are able to connect in a deeper way than usual. Those moments are precious. They often come at bedtime or when a child needs comfort, or even in the midst of correction. Pray that God would give you those moments in your day to strengthen the relational bonds. Also take time to pray that God would provide you with teaching opportunities. Often it's a thoughtful comment or a creative idea that connects with a child's heart.

Those often come spontaneously as gifts directly from the Lord. So, take time to pray for insight. God may use your own walk with him to give you an idea, or you may discover a truth in a book you're reading or some advice you overheard. Be on the lookout for tools to teach. Just like any good teacher, you want to always be looking for ideas of ways to bring about the light-bulb moments in the hearts of your children.

The reality is that parenting is the toughest job in the

world. We need all the help we can get. God promises us that we can ask him for wisdom and he'll give it to us. James 1:5 says, "If any of you lacks wisdom, he should ask God, who gives generously to all without finding fault, and it will be given to him." Parenting often brings us to our knees. Sometimes we think we know what we're doing as parents but that feeling of confidence doesn't usually last too long. In fact, our weakness as parents often gives us a greater appreciation of our Heavenly Father who wisely provides guidance, discipline, and strength in just the right measure for us.

During your prayer time take a moment and thank God for his faithfulness to you. One of the greatest gifts we have is to become part of God's family. We are his children if we have trusted Christ as savior. That is an awesome privilege that we enjoy. In fact, you will want to pray regularly that you can help your children understand God's grace in that same way. As you express to your children the appreciation you have for God's love and mercy in your life, your prayer is that they'll see the need to seek God for themselves and develop a personal relationship with Him. When family life gets difficult and you feel stressed by the challenges of the day, remember to go to the Lord for strength.

Psalm 91:1-2 says, "will rest in the shadow of the Almighty. I will say of the LORD, 'He is my refuge and my fortress, my God, in whom I trust.' " We all need rest and a fortress sometimes. God is our strength. Prayer is the vehicle God designed to transport your heart into his presence. Use it often and you'll be a better parent .

Prayer Point

- My seeds shall not be the weakest link in life.

- I exclude my children from rape, from jail, from kidnap, from abduction, from drugs, from terrorists, from every evil pop culture in the world by the blood of Jesus.

- I erase my children's names from the list of the devil.

- My childrens future is safe and secure in the blood of Jesus.

- Every curse of my father's house, and my mother's house, working against my children, break and scatter, in the name of Jesus.

Ways To Pray With Your Kids

Through out the past 50 years there has been a shift from the traditional church structure to a more family oriented body of believers. Though overall this transition has been positive, today there is a lower number of children learning the basics of the Christian faith at church. Churches now rely on parents as the primary instructor of faith; however, many parents feel inadequate in their approach to passing along their beliefs to their children.

Even though, most parents want their children to have a solid foundation in their faith, they do not know how to make that connection. The goal of this chapter is to help believers close the gap between their faith and their children.

Let Your Children See And Hear You Pray

It is also important that you pray aloud when your children are around. Anytime a situation arises that evokes prayer take time to pray and involve your children in it. Whether it be an illness, financial difficulty, loss, etc., children take note and will learn to use prayer in the same way.

Talk About Prayer

You should also talk to your children about prayer. Give your children a simple explanation about prayer avoiding deep theological language. It opens up dialogue and allows your children to ask about the super natural.

Pray Intentionally

Also, look for opportunities to pray. Be mindful of the affect your prayers will have on your children and intentionally use opportunities to teach them about prayer. The more a child sees his or her parent praying the more the child is apt to pray in similar situations.

Pray Often

Finally, pray with your children throughout the day, not just at bedtime. Some of the greatest times to pray include before school and before meals. By setting a routine children will want to continue that routine on their own.

Prayer Point

- I decree that my children are supremely blessed.
- My children will be at the highest ranking of the land, highest ranking of their education and their careers.
- I pray that the anointing and the power to be supremely blessed be placed upon my children.
- Every cause of evil family pattern in my children, be nullified by the blood of Jesus
- Every cause of transferred virtues in my childrens life, be nullified by the blood of Jesus.
- Every cause of being pursued by the spirit of death in my childrens life, be nullified by the blood of Jesus.
- Every curse by known and unknown persons, be revoked by the blood of Jesus.

Powerful Prayers For Children

Prayer for their money, wealth and work

We want our children to have a healthy relationship with money, understanding that wealth is not equated to a person's worth nor do they bring ultimate happiness. We want them to understand that the things of this world can bring us enjoyment, but that lasting joy is found only in God.

Heavenly Father, help us to model a healthy example of how to handle possessions and money. Help us to work hard, but to not wear ourselves out in order to get rich so that our children can witness a positive, godly view of hard work and the pursuit of success.

Prayer for their health

Exodus 23 verse 25 to 26, "So you shall serve the Lord your God, and He will bless your bread and your water. And I will take sickness away from the midst of you. No one shall suffer miscarriage or be barren in your land; I will fulfill the number of your days."

Father, just as you have promised in your word, I pray that sickness and diseases will be far from my children in Jesus Name. I pray that I shall not bury any of my children. By your mercy and grace Lord, you will fulfill all their days in Jesus' name.

I pray that you will take this disease away from my child in Jesus' name. And from this moment, she/he will begin to enjoy complete health in Jesus Name.

Prayer for safety and protection

Lord, I commit my children into your hands that they will be protected under your wings. Lord, please be their refuge and their fortress. I pray that no evil shall befall any of my children neither will any plague come near them.

I pray that you will keep them and be with them when they go out and when they come in. You will protect them with your angels in all their ways. I pray that you will be with them in any trouble they find themselves and deliver them out of it. And that you will bless.

Prayer against fear

Lord, the world we live in today is full of fear and uncertainty. But, Lord, I pray that you will help these children to be strong in you. I pray that you will make them as bold as a lion and you be their confidence in Jesus Name.

Prayer to know Christ as the 'All in all'

Father, I pray that my children will know Christ and that they will be able to do all things through Him.

I pray that Christ will be their all in all and they learn to put their complete trust in Him in Jesus Name.

Prayer to have wisdom and understanding

"The fear of the Lord is the beginning of wisdom: all who have His precepts have good understanding." Psalm 111:10.

Father, even a child is known by his actions, whether his deeds are pure and right (Proverbs 20:11). I pray You would grow my children to be known as those who are gentle and kind, bearing much fruit of the Holy Spirit. Where they lack discernment, teach them what is right.

Warfare Prayers For Children

Part of praying for your child is understanding your right to go before the throne and intercede for him or her. You may be certain that if you are trying to live a good life and do something for God, the devil is going to come after either you, your spouse and your children.

Since neither you nor your children are perfect, you need daily appropriate covering of the blood of Jesus for the remission of your sins and theirs before the throne. This "Throne of Power" is a truly awesome weapon in the arsenal of the parent and should never be overlooked. Here are some welfare prayers for your children!

- Father, I come before your throne of mercy in the name of the true God who made heaven and earth, and I come against the pleadings of the devil over my children. I say, "God rebuke thee, Satan" and command that the devil take his hands off my children.
- I declare that although we are not perfect, our righteousness is in the Lord Jesus Christ, and my children are covered in His blood and belong to Jesus the resurrection and the life.
- Father, in the name of Jesus Christ, I come to you desiring my children to be set free from all generational sins, iniquities, and their results, which may have an influence upon my children.

- I claim release and freedom through the blood of the Lord Jesus Christ. I pray that my son/daughter would fear you, and that from now on righteousness would be the heritage of my family, of my children, and of our future generations.
- I pray that my childrens life will bring glory to you, and I ask that you will give me wisdom in training them up in the way you would have them to go. Amen.
- Lord, I pray that my children will receive you as their Saviour at an early age.
- Place within their heart a desire to follow you all the days of their life. Keep them pure and willing to wait until you reveal your life partner for them in your perfect will.

Decree And Declare Over Your Children

Father God I thank you for the gift of children and with the authority and power given to me through Jesus, I prophesy over my children saying:

- My children are generous
- My children are loving
- My children are wise and make great decisions
- My children are kind to all
- My children are heavily protected
- My children , give their best at Whatever they do

- My children are highly favoured by God and man
- My children are exactly where they need to be at the right time and right place
- My children are Blessed
- My children are healthy and wealthy
- My children are united and peaceful
- My children find creative solutions to any problems or challenges they face
- My children are GOD fearing
- My children bear the fruits of the Holy Spirit
- My children are obedient and respectful.

Julian Businge

Chapter 9

Inspiring Stories

Love Stories That Inspires

A story from Crystal

My name is Crystal and I'm here to let you know that with man it may seem impossiblebut with Almighty God, nothing is impossible. I made a promise to God and to myself that when he restored my marriage, I would testify and tell the world. I would share EVERY single detail no matter how shameful and embarrassing it would be, in the hope and knowledge that I would someday be able to bring some kind of hope for a hurting wife or husband who would've been going through what I once was.

I'll try to be as brief as possible but I really don't want to leave any detail out no matter how small, because it may be the very thing God wants to use to inspire and encourage a stander or prodigal spouse. I don't want to apportion blame too much here but suffice it to say we had some in-law issues which contributed greatly to our demise but that is another story and I want to concentrate on how God showed up and showed off in the mist of my situation.

Today is March 16th 2011. My husband of 1 year and 5 months left me on November 30th, 2010 but all thanks and all praise be to Almighty God, he is now back home and we are rebuilding a marriage that from all counts and to the naked eye in the natural realm was dead.

As far as I could see we were the perfect couple: we went out together, stayed home together, laughed, and joked together. We were like two peas in a pod. Of course we had our regular marital problem. No marriage is perfect. In addition to the above, we also argued and sometimes told each other some harsh words like every other couple. It wasn't right but it happened. In spite of all this , I believed he loved me just as much as I loved him. You could imagine my surprise and heart break when one day after a short disagreement, and I mean short lasting no more that a few minutes, my beloved husband packed his clothes and walked out of my life.

All this happened on 30th November 2010. I held off from calling him because I was still upset and I figured I didn't do him any harm. He was the one that stepped out in our marriage and on our marriage. Ours wasn't a physical stepping as in outside sex it was an on-going 5 month relationship on the internet, with someone he had been previously involved with. The days went by and he didn't call so on 5th December 2010, I called him. He refused to take my calls so I texted him only to be told that he wasn't interested in me and I should go on with my life. He wrote that I should never call or text him again. This was like a dagger through my heart. I felt as though someone had literally ran a knife straight through my stomach and was twisting it repeatedly but that isn't the worse yet.

I persisted in calling him that same day and eventually he picked up the phone. He was as cold as ice. I felt frightened even listening to him. He told me: *I never loved you. I am sorry we got married. I felt trapped in this marriage. I don't love you like a man should love a woman. The feelings I have for you is that of a "good" friend. I don't want to be with you and you should get on with your life. I'm not coming back.*

I have never felt pain like I did then in my entire life. It is amazing when you are down on luck how quickly you remember that GOD does exists. I was a regular church goer and I tithed but I still didn't have that personal relationship with God. Well God has a way of getting our attention in ways unimaginable and he got mine.

I cried daily and hourly. I felt all hope was gone. I mean how do you get someone to love you again when that person is saying I never loved you at all. You can't but God can. I had built my life around my husband and now he was gone. I felt like I lost the better part of me. I couldn't eat. I couldn't eat . I didn't want to socialize and I forced myself to go to work but God had a plan even though all seemed lost. God was turning my situation around even as I was hurting. What the devil meant for evil God was turning around for good.

I enlisted the help of three persons: a Prophetess, an Apostle, and a church Pastor. These were the spiritual people I knew and strong men and women of God. I knew I wasn't strong in my spirit and my faith was way less than even that of a mustard seed. I still cried every day but I also engaged in some radical and spiritual warfare for my husband. I spoke the word of God over my marriage everyday and I prayed hedges of thorns around my husband everyday. I pleaded the blood of Jesus over him and claimed my marriage in the name of Jesus.

Remember I wasn't rooted in God so my prayers were not flowing as other people but everyday I gain more and more strength and my faith began to soar. I prayed that God would soften my husband's heart and remind him of the love we once shared. I asked God to send Godly people in his life to speak to him even when I couldn't and God heard me.

I think I either bought or borrowed every book on marriage, warfare, prayer, you name it. I visited every website I could think of. I just wrapped my husband up and prayed what ever prayer I could even verbatim from some of those same books. I became like a one man army. At times the devil whispered in my ears and unbelief and doubt settled in. I would call my prayer warriors for encouragement and go to God crying and in a few hours would be right as rain and ready again to go up against the gates of hell for my boo.

To make a long story short, on Sunday 16th January 2011, I got a text from my husband stating that he wanted to talk and wanted to know if he could come by the house. He wanted to know if I could forgive him for what he did and for us to try again at our marriage. I had released my husband and my marriage to God and I knew God was going to do something but I thought it would be perhaps a 'Hi hello…How are you or perhaps a few weeks down the line he might drop in a call or something'. I had no idea that MY GOD was bringing my husband home that day.

He told me that after he had spoken to me on Thursday, he went to God himself and talked to him and asked him to speak and show him what he should do. He said from the time he said that everything just went crazy. Everything he saw reminded him of me. When he went to sleep, his dreams were constant replays of our life together. He started thinking about stuff that happened before and after our marriage that were nothing short of miraculous. In short, God was speaking to him all along but he was too proud to just walk back and admit that he was wrong. He wanted to give our marriage a chance and he loved me and wanted to be with ME.

I give all the thanks and praise to God for what he did. It doesn't matter what your situation looks like. It doesn't matter how impossible and dead it seems. It doesn't matter what your husband or wife is planning. We plan but God is also planning and he works EVERYTHING out together for those that love the LORD.

Do not give up the devil and even your own mind is going to try to tell you to move on. Leave him/her alone. He/she doesn't want you. There is nothing you can do. There is no one that can help you now. Do not listen even in your tears, cry out to God. When you don't know what to say, just say JESUS. Nothing more. Tears is a language God understands and he is going to work it out. This isn't every single detail of what happened there are parts missing...but my short journey has been nothing but incredible and miraculous but I want you to know that with God ALL THINGS ARE POSSIBLE.

A story from Kami

In March of 2018, I found out my wife had cheated on me. I instantly thanked her for telling me the truth and forgave her, telling her we could work through this and that I loved her.

During the next few days and on one particular day she was screaming yelling and cursing at me really hurtful words which turned into an argument and I left to my parents house because I needed time to process everything.

A couple days later, I came home and the guy she cheated on me with was inside my house with my wife and children and she had him change the locks so I couldn't get in. I continued to stay at my parents while my wife was lying about continuing to see him and eventually when I found the truth out I filed for a divorce. I sought the Lord heavily, after about a month I could not divorce my wife.

I eventually found out that she got an incurable STD from him. I went to war for my wife, praying like I never had before, searching everywhere for prayers like crazy. After about 2-3 months I forgave my wife again of everything and moved back in.

Over the course of the next few months my wife was regularly going out multiple times a week and not coming home until 5 or 6 o'clock in the morning sometimes not until the afternoon. She would regularly show up with bruises all over her body one time even on her neck. We had regular arguments about it and she would not stop.

Eventually I left and went back to my parents house. She is currently sleeping with other men and bringing them around our children which I have 70% of the time. I'm still going to war for my wife although not nearly as heavily as before, maybe 10-20% in comparison.

I feel drained and broken in spirit most days. Jesus never gave up on the church and if I am to follow his lead I won't give up on my wife. This is a spiritual battle. And I need to exhaust every avenue.

About a year before she cheated God sent me a dream showing me that she was going to cheat on me and after a period of ten years (10 is a time of testing) her and I would be reunited. In the dream I saw her in the future and she was beautiful, more beautiful than I have ever seen her and she looked at me with so much love in her eyes it still makes me teary when I recall it.

God has remained faithful to his word and has strengthened me through this whole thing and following his lead I have remained faithful to my wife.

Conclusion

This book is for you all couples who value their marriages no matter what life's experiences you may have gone through the best is yet to come. Am trusting God with you for a blissful marriage.

The Lord will remember you for good and make things work in your favour this day. All shall be well with you. You shall be at peace. You shall eat in satisfaction. Your labour shall be favoured to prosper you. Your hands are blessed to carry prosperity. Your legs are blessed to take you to a place of recognition and honour.

Your mouth is blessed to share wonderful testimonies. Your eyes are blessed to behold and witness the goodness of the Lord. Your marriage is blessed to be fruitful, your home is blessed to carry the glory of the Lord, your work is blessed to be enlarged and expand.

Your life is blessed to change for the best. All that is yours are blessed to give you peace of mind. Never will you have any reason to bow your head in shame this day. You will excel greatly in all you do this day. The Lord shall put permanent stop to all that trouble you, to all that afflict you, to all that give you sleepless night, to all that gives you pain, to all that make you shed silent and secret tears, to all that mock you, to all that ridicule you, to all that belittle you, to all your challenges, to all that intimidate you.

INCREASE YOUR CASH FLOW

SERVICED ACCOMMODATION

JULIAN BUSINGE

About The Author

Julian Businge born and raised in Uganda. She came to the UK to join her husband and start their family. She is an Award winning motivational speaker and Author of **Increase Your Cash Flow: Serviced Accommodation**. She has co-authored many other books such as **Jesus Changed Our Lives** and **Les Brown Changed Our Lives**. She is a certified property and business coach who regularly hosts live property workshops and trainings.

Julian Businge is also a the CEO of Peace Property Education and co-founder of Peace Apartments that provides short-term accommodation in Luton, UK.

More than anything else, Julian is a child of God and happily married with children.

Giving Back

Blessed Hill Children's Centre is an organization designed to support, educate, feed and house orphaned, abandoned and rejected children in Uganda. In 2016, I had the chance to visit this orphanage and I witnessed their daily struggles. My dream is to support this orphanage by establishing a bakery which will enable children to learn the life skill of baking. It is my hope that this will promote their economic independence and empowerment for when they leave the orphanage.

For every copy of this book sold, I will be donating £1 towards the building project of a bakery and all the facilities needed for it to function properly. If you wish to discuss this opportunity further, please email and together we can make a difference to the orphans living in Uganda. My email is info@julianbusinge.com

What Now?

Seek a close relationship with the God of the Bible through the Lord Jesus. Dear Lord Jesus, thank you for dying on the cross for my sin. Please forgive me. Come into my life. I receive You as my Lord and Saviour. Now, help me to live for you the rest of this life. In the name of Jesus, I pray. Amen.

Complete all the tasks, there's still time to bring results to your relationship. Don't under estimate the power of implementing them, a happy marriage takes work.

Keep in touch with us through social media, website. hearing your feedback, testimonies, experiences from you would make my day fabulous and help me serve you better.in this way, you will also stay informed of what we are up to, events around the world.

Do something nice for some one else by giving them a copy of this book. If someone you know is about to get married and needs to learn to do things the right way, get them a copy.

Re read this book in six months. change takes time and requires persistence.so, go to your calendar now and make this note six months from today. It takes a decision to rewrite the future of your marriage.

Julian Businge

Has this book helped you?

Spread the word

Let us know on

Email us at : info@julianbusinge.com

Breakthrough Declarations

www.ingramcontent.com/pod-product-compliance
Lightning Source LLC
LaVergne TN
LVHW051628080426

835511LV00016B/2242